BLACK PEARLS
BOOK OF LOVE

Also by Eric V. Copage:

Kwanzaa: An African Celebration of Culture and Cooking
Black Pearls
Black Pearls Journal
Black Pearls for Parents
A Kwanzaa Fable

BLACK PEARLS
BOOK OF LOVE

Romantic Meditations
and Inspirations
for African Americans

ERIC V. COPAGE

QUILL
WILLIAM MORROW
NEW YORK

Copyright © 1996 by Eric V. Copage

Permissions, constituting a continuation of the copyright page, appear
on page 167.

It is the policy of William Morrow and Company, Inc., and its imprints
and affiliates, recognizing the importance of preserving what has been
written, to print the books we publish on acid-free paper, and we exert
our best efforts to that end.

Library of Congress Cataloging-in-Publication Data

Copage, Eric V.
    Black pearls book of love : romantic meditations and inspirations
for African Americans / Eric V. Copage.
        p.   cm.
    ISBN 0-688-13970-1
    1. Love—Literary collections. 2. Literature—Black authors.
I. Title.
PN8071.L7C67   1996 95-46094
                                                    CIP

Printed in the United States of America

First Quill Edition

1 2 3 4 5 6 7 8 9 10

BOOK DESIGN BY ELIZABETH VAN ITALLIE

To my son, Evan, and my daughter, Siobhán:
May you both find true and everlasting love.

ACKNOWLEDGMENTS

There is an African saying: It takes a whole village to raise a child. Well, the same can be said of writing a book, especially when elements of the book come from disparate sources. And so I would like to acknowledge—and thank—the "village" that helped me make this book a reality.

Thanks to Jack Rosenthal and Adam Moss, the Editor and Editorial Director of *The New York Times Magazine*, for their support while I was working on this book. Thanks to the many friends and friends of friends who shared their memories and feelings about romance with me. Thanks to Deborah Murphy, whose thorough research gave this book its firm foundation. Thanks to Doris Cooper, for her additional research, help in acquiring permissions, keen editorial comments, and overall hard work. And thanks to my editor, Will Schwalbe, who helped me develop my original vision of this work. Last, thanks to my father, who didn't have anything directly to do with this book, but whose life-giving expressions of love and confidence have helped to sustain me and fortify me my entire life.

INTRODUCTION

MY FIRST LOVE was a girl named Karen, who lived down the block from me. We were both about six years old. We played a game called John and Alibe, the names of my parents. This took place around 1960, so, as the father, I went to work, took out the trash, and attended to all the mechanical things around our imaginary Los Angeles home; Karen stayed home, shopped, cooked, and took care of the kids. It was a golden time, and I thought that black love—the love of my parents, the love of her parents, and my puppy love for her—would be as constant as the orbit of the planets and that the radiance of this black love would illuminate our lives forever.

But Karen and I grew apart, as boys and girls are wont to do. I might not have noted our separation, except for my parents' divorce, which happened when I was eight years old. That parting shook my world to its foundations and made me aware that love can indeed come to an end.

As I plowed through junior high, high school, college, and eventually through the work world, I suffered passions of various intensities, some requited, some not. I felt the sting of love's melancholia, anger, sarcasm, irony, and ennui as well as the balm of its humor, peace, elation, romantic eroticism, and bawdiness. As I matured into adulthood, I came to see love in the light of the vagaries, contradictions, stresses, hopes, and desires that comprise the latticework of real intimacy.

The *Black Pearls Book of Love* is a celebration of the complexity of black love, a love made more textured than most by the social pressures militating against it and a centuries-long campaign by others to define it. In this book, black love will speak for itself; it will be allowed to speak in its fullness. Black love is tender. Black love is strong. Black love is sometimes ill defined. Other times black love is as precise as the blade of a surgical knife. To give some sense of the joyful chaos of black love, I have incorporated material from a number of sources: quotes from the famous and the obscure on different aspects of love; charms and fetishes meant to affect love in some manner; folk tales illustrating the humor, magic, and mystery of black love; poetry and prose proclaiming the power of the physical expression of love.

The book is divided into three sections—Finding Love, Keeping Love, Celebrating Love—yet, in keeping with the book's kaleido-scopic approach to love, you needn't read it in that order. Dip into it. Graze. Treat it the way you would an old friend—a seventy-, eighty-, or ninety-year-old—whom you'd call to garner a shard of timeless wisdom one moment, a wry story the next, and another time a bit of practical advice. You can open the pages at random, rifle through, and let the book tell you what you need to read. The theme will come through loud and clear: Black love is a powerful love. It is the love of our parents, of our grandparents—of the primordial African couple millions of years ago. From this love sprang the wealth of our culture—our dance, our music, our speech, our genius. It is the love that gave us the strength to endure our tribula-tions throughout the world for generations. It is the love we pass on to our brothers and sisters, aunts and uncles, nieces and nephews, and most of all our children.

—ERIC V. COPAGE

"LOVE IS THE KEY TO THE SOLUTION OF THE PROBLEMS OF THE WORLD."

—DR. MARTIN LUTHER KING, JR.
NOBEL PRIZE LECTURE
DECEMBER 11, 1968

FINDING LOVE

THERE ARE JOYS in finding true love, but there are challenges also, especially when you are looking for love the second or third time around. There are emotional issues: insecurities and fears of becoming vulnerable again, fears of rejection. There is also the fear that you might already have missed Mr. or Ms. Right. This latter fear is understandable if you believe the statistic that you have to meet at least two hundred people before finding one with whom you are even remotely compatible. A friend of mine figured that if he met one new person each and every single day—he defined the word *meet* as spending at least a half hour with somebody over coffee or drinks—it would take over six months to find the woman of his dreams. And who meets a new person a day for weeks on end, anyway?

I think my friend might be too scientific, but it's true that throughout the ages and around the world people seem to have realized that they are fighting formidable odds, and therefore have employed a wide variety of resources to inspire them and give them strength and hope in their quest for love. In the following section I've included charms and spells from the streets of New Orleans and the sunny ports of the Caribbean as well as personal ads from papers in South Africa. I've included philosophies and cautionary notes about finding love, and an African folktale about a kind of love that is literally magic, sometimes attained by trickery, other times awarded on merit. I've included quotes on how to recognize love when you find it. And of course I've included poems and ruminations about the hunt for love—the longing, the anticipation, the confusion, and finally the satisfaction upon finding it.

Ten Ways to Find Love

1. Have a party 2. Dare to be a blind date 3. Attend a concert alone or with a friend of the same sex 4. Enroll in a night class 5. Don't be overly judgmental 6. Flirt 7. Put an ad in the personals section of your newspaper 8. Tell friends you're looking for love 9. Keep an open mind 10. Love yourself

COME. AND BE MY BABY

The highway is full of big cars
going nowhere fast
And folks is smoking anything that'll burn
Some people wrap their lives around a cocktail glass
And you sit wondering
where you're going to turn.
I got it.
Come. And be my baby.

Some prophets say the world is gonna end tomorrow
But others say we've got a week or two
The paper is full of every kind of blooming horror
And you sit wondering
What you're gonna do.
I got it.
Come. And be my baby.

MAYA ANGELOU

APHRODISIAC:

Boil together marbay bark, anise seeds, and nutmeg mace (skin covering the nutmeg shell). Sweeten with sugar and drink a wineglass of it every day.

—TRINIDAD

A WOMAN WHO KNOWS HOW TO COOK IS MIGHTY PRETTY.

—Jamaican proverb

" BEFORE thinking
about getting married, or even living with one
another, it is important to live on your own.
Living on your own, you discover how to man-
age a whole range of household duties: cooking,
shopping, cleaning, fixing things, and making a
living. Once you have confidence in yourself that
you can do whatever is needed to live in this
world, then you can look for the right mate—a
partner, rather than a mother or father substitute, or someone to fill in your deficiencies."
— RICHARD J., AGE FORTY, BUS DRIVER,
CINCINNATI

THE BIRD PRINCE

Once upon a time there was a girl who went out one fine day in search of a mimosa tree. These mimosa trees produce a sweet gum that is considered a delicacy in Botswana. She walked and walked until the sun set and she did not recognize the landscape. She was lost! Fortunately she saw smoke rising in the desert, and as you know, where there is smoke, there is fire, and if fire is not made by lightning, it is made by people. So the girl walked in the direction of the smoke until she found an old woman sitting in front of her hut and cooking her porridge.

The girl greeted her politely and asked if she could help, for she saw that the woman had only one arm. The old woman took a liking to her, and that was her good luck, for little did she know yet that she would owe her life to her own politeness. Courtesy costs crumbs, as they say, which means it's cheap, considering what you can get for it sometimes!

The old woman said, "It is too late for you to go back now, it will soon be night. You could not have been more unlucky: this is the house of a *demo*, a giant cannibal who will come home in a short while. Now, listen carefully, for I like you and I will help you to survive.

"The giant will put a spell on you as soon as he comes home so that you cannot run away unless you rub your head with the magic powder from the white calabash that he has in his sleeping cabin. He will invite you there tonight. Go with him, but instead of the white calabash, which he will order you to get him, give him the brown calabash. The powder in it will put him to sleep as soon as he has rubbed his head with it. In the darkness he will not be able to see the difference between white and brown, as his eyes are not very good. Remember, do not touch the powder from the brown calabash, it is poison!"

No sooner had she finished than a rumbling like thunder was heard and there appeared the giant, humming cheerfully to himself. It was this humming that sounded like thunder. He shouted, "Here old woman, I had some luck in my hunting today. Cook one of these for my supper tonight so I won't have to eat your other arm tonight. Ha ha ha!"

While his laughing made the trees tremble, he threw down the dead bodies of a man and a woman who had failed to escape him. At that moment he discovered the girl, who had tried to sit as far away from the fire as possible.

"Ha ha! Who have we here?" he thundered, "a little woman of the men! You are lucky I don't have to eat you tonight, I have food enough just now, I will eat you later when my storeroom is empty. You can't escape anyway. Ha ha! Fancy such a morsel just walking into my frontyard. My lucky day it is!"

Meanwhile the body of one of the two people was roasting over the fire and the smell of burning flesh seemed to delight the giant. He picked the body up and began to devour it as if it were a fried chicken, tearing off limbs and crunching the bones with his long lion's teeth. Remember that cannibals are recognizable by their dentures.

The old woman meanwhile shared her porridge with the girl. She was used to the sight of people finding their graves in the demo's mouth, but the girl, I don't have to tell you, could not swallow half a mouthful while she heard and smelled the consumption of a fellow human being.

Finally, the giant retired for the night, taking the girl with him. She could not escape. He told her to bring him the white calabash, so she brought him the brown one. He shook some powder into his hand and rubbed his head with it. Soon he fell into a deep sleep. The girl took the brown calabash and poured out all the powder over his head, to make quite sure he would sleep for a long time. Then she took the white calabash, rubbed her own head with some of the powder in it, and suddenly she felt quite refreshed.

She decided to run away at once; she thanked the old woman

and quickly ran away over the hills and down into the valley, over which the rising moon poured its light like fresh milk. She did not really know where she was going, she just ran, and when she was tired, she walked farther until she saw the first red streak of dawn between the sky and the horizon. Suddenly she heard behind her a familiar rumbling noise: it was the giant whom the fresh morning air had aroused from his deep sleep. One of his steps covered as much distance as ten of the girl's steps.

In the middle of the plain near the river's edge there stood an enormous tree. The girl ran and ran. When she reached the tree, she climbed up in it. *Demos* cannot climb, that is a well-known fact, but this *demo* had nails as big as ax blades and equally sharp. He at once proceeded to chip away at the roots, but it was a big tree, so it took him some time, even with his ten nail-blades. Meanwhile the girl prayed to the tree to stand upright, and then to the sun to send someone to rescue her. She did not know it, but the sun heard her prayer. Before the tree fell down, there was a flash of sunlight in the sky, and a golden bird appeared, swooped down, and picked her out of the tree as if she were a fruit. He carried her up into the air as if she were a leaf.

The big bird flew with her to his nest up in the mountains. There he put her down on a rocky summit and alighted next to her. Standing up, he was as tall as she was. He looked her in the face, then began to speak to her in human language (literally, the narrator said, "in good Se-Tswana"), thus:

"I have saved your life and now I want you to help me. I am the son of a king and my mother was the sun-god's daughter. We lived in peace and happiness for many years until the land of my father was visited by a man-eating monster that made children into slaves and burned all the huts with its flaming breath. It devoured my father and all the elders of his council. I escaped only because my mother quickly changed herself and me into sunbirds. Ever since, we have been flying around in search of the one person who can liberate our country from this scourge: a brave girl who will agree to marry me no matter what happens. Will you?"

"Yes I will."

The girl did not hesitate. What else could she do? She had no fiancé anyway. So the eagle picked her up again and flew with her to a desert. There in the middle of the desert was a cave, and in the cave there was the monster, fast asleep so that the rock trembled with the snoring. The sun-eagle alighted on top of the rock, having put the girl on her feet first.

He spoke: "Now, here is what you have to do. We will go down to the cavern; there I will put you down on the monster's head. Here is my spear. You have to stab the monster in his neck, just behind the head. If you don't hit it on the right spot, it will wake up and kill you. Now, you can still decide if you do or do not want to do all this. Most girls are not made to handle spears and kill dragons. You can still say no, in which case I will carry you to your parents' home, where you may live in peace forever."

After these solemn words the girl answered, still without hesitation, "I will do it."

The eagle then picked her up and carried her down along the rock face to where, under the huge arch of a cave entrance, the dragon could be seen, still fast asleep. The eagle gently put the girl down on the dragon's big head. She turned to the neck, raised the spear, and thrust it downward so that the point pierced the neck just behind the head. The monster died immediately.

"Well done!" said a well-known voice. When she looked up, she saw not the eagle but a handsome young prince. She had broken his spell by killing the monster. She married him and became the richest queen in Africa.

—SOUTH AFRICA

I MARRIED
TO A MILLIONAIRE

Believe me, I nuh care,
All I know, I married to a
  millionaire.
If him die,
I nah cry,
All I do
Just pop another guy.

— Jamaica

"UNTIL you decide to dedicate yourself to one woman or one man, the two most important words in your vocabulary should be *safe sex*. And, guys, don't be put off if she should offer you a condom from her nightstand. You don't honestly think you are the first person she has slept with? Besides, it's a good bet that if she is giving you a condom, she has given them to other lovers. If that doesn't make you feel especially good, it should make you feel relatively safe." —DOLORES T., AGE TWENTY-THREE, SECRETARY, SEATTLE

African Lonely Hearts

(Letters from the "Lonely Hearts" pages of the *Johannesburg Magazine*, South Africa)

Find Her!

Find me a lady of sober habits. I am 25 and single. At this stage I can only offer to correspond with her, but later anything can happen.

—Timothy

Respect!

People might find it hard to believe that at 18 I have never had a boyfriend, but it is true. Now I would like young boys of my age to write to me. They should be respectable and respectful, otherwise I will not reply to their letters.

—Dolly

16 to 60

Still a bachelor, I'm 23, fond of reading, writing, music, dancing, cycling, and exchanging views. Can't say I've given marriage serious thought, but I'm nuts about girls. I take them from 16 to 60.

—Lady's Man

Loneliest

Being a sewing instructress at the social welfare center, I met a man who promised me all the love that men can give. But when he gave me a baby, he said he was too young to marry and that he wanted to further his studies abroad. From that time I became the loneliest girl in the world. I lost all interest in the cinema or any kind of enjoyment. My child is now three and she is all that matters to me. I now want a man to share my life by corresponding with me. I am a Kikuyu and I would like a man between 25 and 35 years of age. Preferably he should be one who has lost his true love, like myself.

—Lucy

Blues Got Me!

The blues got me, got me bad, sister! I'm 22, a hot number, all set for getting hitched pronto, and no questions. The guy's gotta be 23 to 30, and maybe we could meet, but nothing doing till I've made the contact. Hey, boys?

—Florence

Rhodesian

At 23, I am expecting my second child although I am not married. I have lost faith in the father of my children because he is so inconsiderate and selfish. I wonder if there is a chance of finding a suitable partner (preferably from the Rhodesias) to take me under his wing. The gentleman must be in the age group of 26–30.

—Patricia

Cinematic

Johannesburg is a big city, but somehow I am terribly lonely. I am not a Prince Charming, but then again I am no Frankenstein either. My interests are quite simple—letter writing and going to the cinema. I am 22 years old and would like some teenage girls to write to me. They may smoke as much as they want, but they should not drink. Snaps will be appreciated.

—Abram

Inspirer

Being a student at the age of 25, I need a girl with some interest in me. She must help me and encourage me to be a prominent man in the future. I want to be a doctor and I need an inspirer. This lady should be about 18 to 20 years of age. She must be interested in housekeeping or can take on any other profession if she wants to work. She must remain with my relatives during the school terms. When the schools close, we can have all the happiness that is in the world. When I am away, she must not flirt with other men. I do not drink, gamble, nor dance. I expect my spouse to have the same qualities.

—Isaac

CHARMS AND SPELLS IN LOVE

Human beings are driven to look for that edge. We're all angling for the inside track, whether we're talking about a job promotion, the best place to view a basketball game, or the best deal on a new suit or dress. In love we try for that inside track, also. The most common way is to reconnoiter your love prospect: Get to know his or her friends and find out the favorite drink, favorite color, favorite hangout, favorite activities of your intended. There is also the metaphysical approach: charms, potions and spells. Throughout the book, I've recounted a few of them conjured from the misty folklore of the Caribbean and the American South.

Ed Murphy suggests the chewing of "heart's root" to soften a person's heart, either in making trades or in courting, while Frank Dickerson thinks "shame-weed" (the sensitive plant—a species of vetch) root is better. Chew this latter, spit it on your hands, and shake hands with the person whom you want to win. Or prick your finger (the third finger on your left hand) with a pin, take some of the blood, and write your name and your sweetheart's name on a piece of paper. Draw a heart around the names and bury the paper under your doorstep. Your absent lover will return to you at once. Else, simply rub lizard dust on your lover's head. Or, if you like, you may win a person's affections by giving him wine in which your nail trimmings have been soaked.

—LOUISIANA VOODOO PRACTICE

TO MAKE PEOPLE LOVE YOU

Take nine lumps of starch, nine of sugar, nine tea-spoons of steel dust. Wet it all with Jockey Club cologne. Take nine pieces of ribbon, blue, red, or yellow. Take a dessertspoonful and put it on a piece of ribbon and tie it in a bag. As each fold is gathered together, call his name. As you wrap it with yellow thread, call his name till you finish. Make nine bags and place them under a rug, behind an armoire, under a step or over a door. They will love you and give you everything they can get. Distance makes no difference. Your mind is talking to his mind and nothing beats that. — FLORIDA FOLK BELIEF

TO MAKE A LOVE POWDER

Gut live hummingbirds. Dry the heart and powder it. Sprinkle the powder on the person you desire.

— LOUISIANA FOLK BELIEF

The thing about first dates is that they are almost always

exhilarating. You have gone through prescreening—the half-hour to hour predate lunch or drinks during which you have decided you can spend an entire evening together—and now comes the moment of truth. It is time to do your high-wire act: on the one hand you want to be on your best behavior, but on the other hand you don't want to be phony. And the strange thing is, you may not be able to tell your true reactions.

The first date is a time when you are ultrasensitive to the reactions of

your date and are trying to interpret them accurately. When you mentioned that you are divorced and he leaned back in his chair, did that mean he was no longer interested in you, or did it mean he was simply tired of leaning forward? When she showed you a passage of a magazine she was reading while waiting for you to arrive at the theater, did she do it so that the two of you could "accidentally" touch shoulders, or did she really think the item was interesting?

The first date is a time to show how well you were listening during the

predate. A colleague of mine remembered that during get-acquainted drinks, his lady friend mentioned that she was fascinated by hands. For their first date he took her to a restaurant that featured palm reading. Another colleague, during a quick predate sandwich, told the woman he was lunching with that she had the graceful movements of a cat. She replied that to the extent she was graceful at all, she saw herself more as a dolphin. For their first date he took her to an aquarium.

During the first date you are still getting to know each other, so you

want to allow enough time to talk. That means if you go to a movie, allow enough time before or after to talk, either while walking around an interesting place in your town or at a restaurant. And since it is only the first date, whether the man pays or you go Dutch, you want to keep it relatively cheap. After all, you two are not going to pledge your undying love tonight. During the summer some cities have outdoor plays and movies that are free. Look in your local paper for events that are free or inexpensive: kite-flying contests, parades, street fairs.

Here are five interesting places to have a first date (but remember, the magic is not in the place but in the chemistry of the two of you and in your ability to listen):

1. Anytime: dinner or drinks in a restaurant located at the top of a tall building in your town so that you have a spectacular view. (This is especially good after a movie.) Restaurants with lots of candlelight are also good.

2. In summer, go ice-skating in a year-round ice rink. (Obviously you can go ice-skating anytime in a year-round rink, but it's least expected in the summer.)

3. In winter, go to the tropical plant pavilion at the botanical garden. (Again, you can do this anytime, but it's least expected in the winter.)

4. Go rowboating, or have a picnic in the park.

5. Visit the aquarium or a zoo. Even if your girlfriend or boyfriend doesn't empathize with the grace of dolphins, it's still a great place for a date. There are enough interesting things to look at, yet there is still plenty of opportunity to talk and get to know each other better.

TO WIN LOVE

• Wrap a thimble in a small piece of silk and carry this in your pocket for three days. Every time you enter or leave the house, make a wish regarding your sweetheart. Your wish will come true in three months.

• Place the man's picture behind a mirror.

• Write the man's name and yours on separate pieces of paper. Pin them together in the form of a cross with yours on top. Put them in a glass of water containing sugar and orange-flower water and burn a red candle before this glass for nine days.

TO WIN LOVE

• Take some of the desired one's hair and sleep with it under the pillow.

• Carry a piece of weed called John the Conqueror in your pocket.

• Rub love oil into the palm of your right hand.

"ANYONE
CAN HAVE SEX,
BUT NOT
EVERYONE
CAN BE
ROMANTIC."

—TYRA BANKS

Nothing on Earth Is Cleverer Than the Female Sex

See, my grandchild! As I teach you, and you children in the older class teach each other, you think, *We men are clever.* If you see womankind and watch how four or five of them sit together and tell each other things, you think, *Instead of chatting here, they ought to get up, go home and cut grass.* As you talk like this to each other, you think in your own minds, *They are stupid and ignorant.* See, my grandchild, they are not stupid. Nothing in the whole world is cleverer than the female sex. Know this, if you are as other men, you are not as intelligent as a woman. It is only that she is given into your charge. If it were you who were given into her charge, she would surpass you in intelligence. Therefore I tell you, a woman will hold a thing in her head better than you. See, my grandson, you live together and she is your wife. Drive a cow into the house and let her milk it. Now, if you feel a bit hungry during the night, because you have not eaten your fill, then you say to her, "If only you had cooked a milk dish, we would have easily eaten our fill!" And she says to you, "Oh, no, there was not enough to cook a dish with. Get some more!"

See, my grandson, you must realize that a woman is intelligent. For she wants to keep the milk until it is sour, so that when she puts it into the food, it is strong enough to give a good taste to it. But you just listen and say nothing. The next day, when the sun rises, she says to you, "Help me and put out a piece of banana branch for the cow, so that it can chew it slowly, while I go to fetch grass." Then while you are cutting that piece of banana branch, you think, *All right, I'll examine the calabash to see whether she was deceiving me when she said there was no more milk in it, or if there really isn't any in it.* When you have cut the piece of banana branch, you seize the calabash, you pick it up like that and then put it down again. You don't drink any of it, Oh, no! When she comes, you say nothing, get up and go out to where the men are. See, my grandson, the woman seeks out the calabash and thinks, *I wonder whether when he had cut the piece of banana branch, he took up and looked at the calabash?* She goes, finds it, and notices that you have turned it around, put it down in another position, and were unable to set it down as she did.

If you do this four times, the woman will speak of it behind your back. Then if you are a little rude to her, she will go to her family; and if you and they then discuss the matter, and the woman is not properly trained—no one has told her "You must not say such things"—her education having been neglected, she says, "Get up and go away from here, monster, you who lift up women's calabashes." With such words she brings you into great disrepute and you are hated among men. They curse you and say, "What is the point of touching women's calabashes?" And the women speak of you and say, "I should not like to be married to a man who lifts women's calabashes!"

See, my grandson, as a man you are not capable of setting down anything anywhere so that you can see, as a woman can, whether it has been touched.

Therefore I tell you, a woman is clever. And if you respect what is women's business, your reputation will not suffer. And your wife will honor you, because she knows that you have learned to keep quiet like other men.

—TANZANIA

The Serving Girl

The calabash wherein she served my food
Was polished and smooth as sandalwood.
Fish, white as the foam of the sea,
Peppered and golden-fried for me.
She brought palm wine that carelessly slips
From the sleeping palm tree's honeyed lips.
But who can guess, or even surmise
The countless things she served with her eyes?

—Aquah Laluah

"He says
he knew I was
the girl for
him when he
saw me
smother my
French fries in
hot sauce."

—Holly Robinson about
her husband, Philadelphia Eagles backup
quarterback Rodney Peete

TACUMA WINS THE GIRL

Anancy and Tacuma were very good friends, and they always fren' *one girl*—both of dem friendly with one girl. Anyone that the girl love most, well, she will get 'im. So they went on and went on, every evenin' visiting this girl, until di girl said to dem, "Any one of you that have the mos' money, I will marry."

Anancy scrape up every farthin' dat him have put in him jar—*big jar* of pure checks. What you tink Tacuma do? Full his jar of mess, dirt, mess! Because he didn' have any money. And the two of dem start out now, and when they journey, hear di Tacuma to Anancy: "Bredder Anancy, I would like you to marry dat girl, you know, [plaintively] for I can't support him."

"[nasally] Certainly."

"You give me your jar and tek my jar."

The idiot Anancy go ahead and say all right, give Tacuma his jar of pure checks and tek Tacuma jar of mess! And them go in the home now, and when dem go in the home and dem put down dem jar on di table, and them come to business now, fi check money; di girl tek Tacuma money first what he took from Anancy, and open it: oh, pure checks! She *laugh* and so pleased, and she put it one side. And when she came to Tacuma's, she say well this must be gold, it is so heavy. When she open, pure *mess*! She flash it outside, my dear! And dat was Tacuma money, you know; and she laugh now over Anancy money, thought that Tacuma would have more, and she didn' know that a swap dem swap by the way, and she dash it outside, and run out poor Anancy, and tek Tacuma now wid Anancy pot of checks.

So Anancy go outside, and Tacuma married the girl—with his money.

—JAMAICA

MAMMA'S DARLING

Wid flowers on my shoulders,
An' wid slippers on my feet;
I'se my mammy's darlin',
Don't you think I'se sweet?

I wish I had a fourpence,
Den I mought use a dime.
I wish I had a Sweetheart,
To kiss me all de time.

I has apples on de table,
An' I has peaches on de shelf;
But I wish I had a husband—
I'se so tired stayin' to myself.

—AFRICAN-AMERICAN FOLK RHYME

MY BROTHERS

my brothers i will not tell you
who to love or not love
i will only say to you
that
Black women have not been
loved enough.

i will say to you
that
we are at war & that
Black men in america are
being removed from the
earth
like loose sand in a wind storm
and that the women Black are
three to each of us.

no
my brothers i will not tell you
who to love or not love
but
i will make you aware of our
self hating and hurting ways.
make you aware of whose bellies
you dropped from.
i will glue your ears to those images
you reflect which are not being
loved.

—HAKI R. MADHUBUTI

A BIT MORE complex is the frog charm.

Kill a frog, dry him thoroughly in the sun (or put him in an ant's bed) until the flesh is all removed from the bones. Among the bones you will find one that looks like a fishhook, another like a fish scale. To win the desired person, hook the bone looking like a fishhook in her garments when the girl (or man) is not looking. She will immediately develop a strong liking for you. In case her extreme devotion proves too irksome, flip the bone looking like a fish scale at her as she walks away. Her love for you will immediately disappear.

Other items used in making love charms are the skin of a "copper-belly" moccasin wrapped around a smoke-dried toad to which two rusty horseshoe nails have been added; a cake made of amaranthe seeds and pounded new wheat; and a white dove's heart swallowed raw with the point downward.

—LOUISIANA VOODOO PRACTICES

"I'VE
FOUND THAT
ROMANCE COMES
DOWN TO SOME
VERY SIMPLE
QUALITIES: YOU
FIND THE PERSON
WHO KNOCKS YOUR
SOCKS OFF AND,
IDEALLY, THE
RELATIONSHIP
BUILDS."

—LIONEL RICHIE

A Woman's Quest

Another story is coming. Stop talking and listen.

There was a very handsome young man, very handsome, and he was called *Dzerikpana*—his public name. Every young lady liked *Dzerikpana*, wanted him, and fell in love with him, but he was fed up with them all. They did not know *Dzerikpana's* birthname, the private one, which was *Dzerikpoli*. Nor did they know where he came from. One day he told his father, *Na*, that there were so many girls who loved him that he did not know which one of them to marry. So he devised a trick. He would lie down and Father *Na* would cover him with a funerary cloth, and tell all the girls that if any of them knew his name, he would marry her. So *Na* covered him, and all the girls in this district were told that their future husband was dead, and if any one of them could weep and call *Dze's* private name, then he would wake up from death and marry that girl. Girls from *Zongo* came, but did not know the right name. Girls from *Saa* also came, but could not succeed. Girls from *Kpagru* came to try, but they failed too. Women from *Tshere* came, but they did not know *Dze's* real name either. Good-time girls from *Wa* also came, but failed. Then one woman, on her way from *Kpongu* to *Busa*, said she would go and say *Dze's* name and marry him because of his handsomeness.

From *Kpongu*, she passed by *Sukpayiri* and walked toward *Nayiri*. On the way, she saw an old woman taking her bath. The old woman said, "My granddaughter," and the young woman greeted her in return. And the old woman said, "Come and wash my back for me before you go." The young woman agreed and went to wash her back, and when she had finished, she said that she had finished. Then the old woman said, "Granddaughter, it is all right! But at *Busa*, there is a man whose name is *Dzerikpoli*." The young woman thanked her for telling her the name of the handsome young man. From there, she started for *Busa* and took the road that passes by the old police station and the chief's farms. On the way to *Busa*, she started her song:

> O Dzerikpoli,
> *I will marry* Dzerikpoli-o!
> O Dzerikpoli, *I will marry* Dzerikpoli.

Dze's father and mother had built a long compound with seven rooms, and kept his corpse in the last, the seventh room, well barred with large doors. As the girl sang *Dze's* private name, the first door swung open. *Dze* could hear her song when she was still at the chief's farm, so he also started his song:

> *Oh, oh, oh, my mother,*
> *Open the doors for me.*
> *Wo, wo, wo, my mother,*
> *Open the doors and let me out.*

Another door opened. On nearing *Kampaha*, the girl sang again:

> O Dzerikpoli,
> *I will marry* Dzerikpoli-o!
> O Dzerikpoli, *I will marry* Dzerikpoli.

The third door opened. The young man heard her, and also repeated his song:

> *Oh, oh, oh, my mother,*
> *Open the doors for me.*
> *Wo, wo, wo, my mother,*
> *Open the doors and let me out.*

And another door was opened, leaving three.

The girl then went some few yards from *Tokoro* hill, and started her song again. *Dze* heard her and again he sang his song. Another door was opened. Now the young woman could see the walls of *Vaara* and started singing again. The good-time girls, on hearing this woman sing *Dze's* name, were all surprised and stood watching her as she approached. Then they stood up and started weeping: "*Wolu, wolu, wolu, wolu*—who is this strange woman from another place who has been able to find out this man's name though we *gentras*, good-time girls, and *tutuhi*, prostitutes, have not been able to know it?" While they were saying all this, the girl sang again, this time louder:

> O Dzerikpoli,
> *I will marry* Dzerikpoli-o!
> O Dzerikpoli, *I will marry* Dzerikpoli.

The young man, now left with two doors to pass through, also sang his song:

> *Oh, oh, oh, my mother,*
> *Open the doors for me.*
> Wo, wo, wo, *my mother,*
> *Open the doors and let me out.*

At this, another door was opened and he was left with one door to pass through. Still, the *Zongo* women, the *Nantiri* women, and the *Wa* prostitutes stood wondering how this woman, who was a stranger, got to know *Dze's* name, and would thus now have the chance of marrying him.

When the woman was a few steps from where *Dze* was, she started her song again:

O Dzerikpoli,
I will marry Dzerikpoli-o!
O Dzerikpoli, *I will marry* Dzerikpoli.

After this, the last door opened and *Dze* came out, and said, "This woman, who has found out my name, she shall be my wife." *Dze* then went and embraced the woman and they started, *kiri,kiri, kiri,* fast toward *Wa.*

On the way, as they were nearing *Kampaha* village, they saw the old woman bathing again. She asked the young woman to come and wash her back, but the young woman, hearing this, turned sharply, and said, "Stop that nonsense! How can I be marrying such a nice young man and come and wash the back of an old woman?"

After this, the two passed by *Kampaha* and, while there, the woman was turned into a leper. At that moment, the young man said, "Why should there be so many beautiful girls and I marry you, a leper?" And then he ran away as fast as he could. Immediately, the leper started, *kpidu, kpidu, kpidu,* running after him. They chased each other until they were in the middle of a thick bush. The man turned into a reed, the type used for making mats laid on by women who have just given birth. The leper turned into a *daangu,* the fiber used to weave the reeds together to make the mats.

A weaver then went to cut the reed and the fiber to weave a mat. After the mat was made, a woman who had just given birth bought it, and while she lay on it, it made some noise, *miu, miu, miu.* This sound shows that the leper has not stopped running after the young man and the young man has also not stopped running.

—WALA, AFRICAN FOLKTALE

VINMOIN
(A ROOT OBTAINED AT THE DRUGSTORE) RUBBED ON ANY PART OF THE PERSON'S BODY WILL ALSO WIN HIS LOVE.

—LOUISIANA VOODOO PRACTICE

SUPERSTITION CONCERNING SAINT ROCH'S

If a young unmarried couple see
their reflections together in the chapel,
they will be married within the year.

—LOUISIANA FOLK BELIEF

CREOLE MIRROR SUPERSTITION

When three men look into a mirror
at once, the youngest is to die; but if
three girls look into a mirror at once,
the eldest will marry within the year.

—LOUISIANA FOLK BELIEF

WINGS OF THE PHOENIX

It was only a dream,
Or so it seemed!
Because we all know,
That love doesn't happen at first sight.
At least not in real life!
Maybe in fairy tales,
And mystical myths
Of fantasy lands
In places far far away
And ages long time gone.
But not for real!
Yet there was that warm,
Dying winter's night
When the dawning of Spring
Was just beyond the horizon,
And the fragrance of freshly bloomed gardenias
Caressed the evening sky.
And I,
Regal and Proud,
Aglow in all my Royal Majesty,
Sailed into the smoke-filled room
That was tinged with the scent
Of freshly harvested herb
And the melodic rhythms
Of Mother Terra's
Most ancient and advanced tribes.
Only to meet
She, for whom my soul has
Eternally longed to greet.
We glanced,
And in that look
All of time ceased,
Eternity unveiled before our eyes,
And we knew that we had always been one!

—NIRVANA REGINALD GAYLE

"**When I was** in my mid-twenties, I was about to get married. I had met my fiancée while waiting in line for a Wynton Marsalis concert to begin. She later told me she had picked me up by offering me my place in line after I had gone off to get a drink of water. I hadn't realized that this was a pickup, but I did see that she was smart, beautiful, and friendly enough. And so we had coffee and then dated. It was a rocky relationship, but, well, I'm shy, you see, and I really didn't think I would ever do any better. So after two years I proposed to her. And she accepted. But we both hemmed and hawed, postponing the wedding date, until finally a job opportunity took her out of the city and we broke our engagement. I was devastated.

"But the break gave me time to wrestle with my shyness. I forced myself to meet women, focusing on them not so much as sexual targets but as potential friends with whom deeper relationships might grow. And I discovered for myself a truism: Everybody is beautiful and unique. The relationships I had after my breakup showed me how special my former fiancée was, yet paradoxically that there were other people with whom I am compatible who are special in different ways. I eventually married another woman, not out of a sense of desperation but for true love and respect. The lesson: If you have any doubts about a marriage, wait. There is plenty of time, and there are plenty of people, even though when you are young— older too, sometimes—it doesn't seem that way."

—WILLIAM H., AGE THIRTY-THREE, ACCOUNTANT, HOUSTON

"I TOOK
ONE LOOK AT
HER AND I
KNEW THAT WAS
THE WOMAN I
WAS GOING TO
MARRY. IT
TOOK ME A
WHILE TO GET
THERE, BUT
I KNEW."

—RON KIRK, FIRST BLACK
MAYOR OF DALLAS, ABOUT HIS WIFE,
MATRIS ELLIS KIRK

A dream of marriage is a sign of death. To dream of death is a sign of marriage. • If, in stirring your tea, the leaves or stalks keep in the middle of your cup, it is a sign that you will soon be married, or talk to a stranger or an absent friend. • If you kiss a boy before you marry, you'll never care very much for him. —AFRICAN-AMERICAN FOLK SUPERSTITIONS

To Discover One's Future Husband: During leap year the girl who counts all the gray (some say white and that a gray mule counts for five horses) horses she sees, until she gets up to a hundred, will be married within the year to the first gentleman with whom she shakes hands after counting the hundredth horse. (Some say she will marry the first man she sees who is wearing a red tie.) To Secure a Husband: Carry an image of Saint Joseph in the purse for six months. On Good Friday one should arise at midnight and look into the mirror in the dark. If you see a face, it is that of your future husband, but if you see a coffin instead, it means you will die soon. —LOUISIANA FOLK BELIEF

HE: De ocean, it's wide; de sea, it's deep.
Yes, in yo' arms I begs to sleep,
Not fer one time, not fer three;
But long as we'uns can agree.

SHE: Please gimme time, Suh, to "reponder";
Please gimme time to "gargalize";
Den 'haps I'll tu'n to "cattlegog,"
An' answer up 'greeable fer a s'prise.

—ANTEBELLUM SLAVE MARRIAGE
PROPOSAL (TRADITIONAL)

"Once, someone came into Chez Josephine—which of course is named for the great star of Paris in the 1920s, Josephine Baker—and wanted to propose to his girlfriend. But he was too nervous, so I had to do it for him. I put them at a lovely table by the window and when the main course came, I served it to them. Underneath the cloche, on a beautiful bed of greens, was the loveliest diamond ring. By then, they didn't eat anything. That cut their appetite."

—JEAN-CLAUDE BAKER,
ADOPTED SON OF JOSEPHINE BAKER
AND OWNER OF JOSEPHINE'S IN
MANHATTAN.

"A GOOD
WOMAN IS
HARD TO FIND.
AND WHEN
YOU FIND ONE,
YOU GOT
TO HOLD ON
TO HER.
WILL YOU
MARRY ME?"

—NFL BACKUP QUARTERBACK RODNEY PEETE
TO TV STAR HOLLY ROBINSON IN FRONT OF A STUDIO
AUDIENCE ON THE SET OF HER SITCOM, "HANGIN'
WITH MR. COOPER"

Gal if yuh love me an yuh no write it
How me fe know?
Gal if yuh love me an yuh no write it
How me fe know?
Gal if yuh write it an me cyaan read it
How me fe know?

Talk it ah mout!
Talk it ah mout!
Talk it ah mout!

—CARIBBEAN FOLK SONG

"I knew something was up when I got to work and found a fantastic bouquet of flowers on my desk. Encircling the vase was a Zulu bracelet of beads, whose colors translated as meaning 'I love you very much.'

"After work I arrived at a wonderful outdoor restaurant where my boyfriend and I arranged to meet. It faced west, so we would see a beautiful sunset on this breezy summer day. When we sat down, he gently held my hand. He seemed about to say something, when the busboy leaned between us, giving us our napkins and silverware. When the busboy left, my boyfriend smiled vaguely, wetted his lips, opened his mouth, and out came the voice of our waitress, who was now standing over us, telling us of the day's special. It seemed that every time my boyfriend was about to gather himself to speak, he would be interrupted: by the serving of appetizers, the arrival of the main course, by refills of water. He was even interrupted by a homeless woman, who snatched two slices of bread from our bread basket, thanking us with a full mouth as she walked away.

"My boyfriend was about to speak again when the waitress came up and asked what we wanted for dessert. My boyfriend put up his hand in a gesture to hold on for just a minute, held my hands with his, looked at me lovingly, and asked me to marry him.

"When I told him yes, the waitress hugged us both and didn't charge us for the dessert."

—BEA R., AGE TWENTY-SEVEN, ADMINISTRATIVE ASSISTANT, BOSTON

BROOM SUPERSTITIONS FROM ISLE BREVILLE

A young couple must not bring an old broom with them into the new house
unless it is thrown in, handle first.
An old couple moving into a new house must bring an old broom.
If they don't, one of them will have bad luck.

—LOUISIANA FOLK BELIEF

A GIRL MARRIES A MONKEY

Here is a story!

(Story it is.)

> Now, on a certain day—
> My story breaks, páá,
> Don't let it break its arms!
> It falls and thuds, wà:à gwò,
> Don't let it break its neck!
> It didn't fall on my head!
> It didn't fall on my neck!
> Nor did it fall on the bit of food
> That I will eat tonight!
> Instead, it fell on the head of a certain woman.

Friends, this woman was so beautiful that I have never seen the like before in my life. You know, her teeth were as white as young palm nuts. Friends, everybody asked to marry her, but she replied it was impossible, she didn't want them. Everyone in the next town and the town after that came to court her. She said, "No," and refused them all. She didn't want them. "Well," her parents asked, "what are we going to do with our daughter?" She said she just hadn't met the right man.

Then one day she went off to the market. Friends, right there her eyes fell on a young man whose skin was as fair as her own. Well, friends, she said, "What luck, thanks to *Olódùmarè* I've seen my future husband at last. I've met him this very day." Then and there she came up behind him and began to follow him around the market. After a while, she knelt down to him, and said, "Hello, master." Friends, hey! He answered, "Thank you, ma." Now, when he noticed her a second time, he laughed in surprise. Oh my! Friends, he repeated, "Thank you, ma, greetings, ma." She continued to follow him. "Is anything wrong?" he asked. "Oh, no! There's nothing wrong at all." "You say there's nothing wrong—nothing?" "Ha! In fact, everything has turned out just right. Oh boy!" "What?" "Thanks be to Ọlọ́run." "Hey, I hope you're not putting me on." "Ha! Is it a put-on that I find you attractive?" "You do?" "You could stop a war with your looks." "You say that?" "We're just like Ẹṣù and Ọyà. Ọlọ́run has planned for us to meet."

Friends, she continued to follow him, she followed along behind, and when it started getting dark, he called, "Hey, friend, stop here. Next time I come, I'll bring money and the rest of the bride price to your mother and father." "Oh, no, that's no good. I don't want to do things like that at all. I'm going with you today. 'One buries the placenta on the same day it appears.' We're both going to my house today!" "Today? Just like that?" "That's right." Well! He had to agree. "It *must* be today." "Yes, okay, I'll go along." "Look, let's go to my parents' house now so you'll know where I live." "Okay," and he followed along behind, kẹ̀ẹ̀ kẹ̀ẹ̀, until they reached her house. He met her mother and prostrated himself in front of her. He greeted her, greeted her mother, and after greeting everyone else, he told them he wanted to marry their daughter. He said she pleased him and he wanted to marry her. They turned to their daughter, "Listen, what do you say about this? Did you hear what this man just said?" "Yes, it's true, I'm prepared to marry him. I really want him to be my husband. I was the one who asked him to come here." Her parents said, "Is that so? We had no idea you were in such a hurry. You have done well."

And since then, girls have been selecting their husbands on their own without waiting for their fathers and mothers to decide. They are the ones who initiate the matter—and trouble along with it. Olódùmarè, don't let us start something that brings us trouble. Amen.

Well, now, friends, mmm, she then announced she was leaving with him right away. "Ha! Can't you wait until tomorrow, can't he come back tomorrow?" No, she wouldn't agree to that. "Well, so long, then." She was really in a hurry—yes, dying with impatience.

Friends, she followed him, walking along behind, yẹ yẹ yẹ yẹ, on and on and on. Huh! Then they got to the end of the street and when they reached the town gate, the man stopped, and surveying her carefully, he advised her to turn back. She replied, "Absolutely not." "If you go back now, I'll come back for you, I'll come meet you. Now get along," he said. Ha! She wouldn't agree. Then he started to plead with the girl, but all she said was, "No." Ha! He said, "Okay, if that's what you want, let's go."

When they had walked about an hour from the town, the man stared up into the sky for a long, long time, and said:

> Àlùfẹ́, *turn around and go back home!*
> > Àlùfẹ́!
> Àlùfẹ́, *turn around and go back home!*
> > Àlùfẹ́!
> Àlùfẹ́, *turn around and go back home!*
> > Àlùfẹ́!
> Àlùfẹ́, *turn around and go back home!*
> > Àlùfẹ́!
> *I'll scramble up a tree and then jump to another,*
> > Àlùfẹ́!
> *When I've jumped to the tree, I'll then jump to a palm,*
> > Àlùfẹ́!
> *And when I've jumped to the palm, I'll jump on a rock,*
> > Àlùfẹ́!
> *Then I'll scamper up and down and shit as I climb,*
> > Àlùfẹ́!
> *I'll scamper with eyes staring white straight ahead,*
> > Àlùfẹ́!
> *I'll scamper some more and bark, "gbóbì,"*
> > Àlùfẹ́!
> *When I've barked, "gbóbì," next I'll bark, "gbágà,"*
> > Àlùfẹ́!
> Àlùfẹ́! *turn around and go back home!*
> > Àlùfẹ́!

Àlùfẹ́,*turn around and go back home!*
Àlùfẹ́,*turn around and go back home!*
Àlùfẹ́,*turn around and go back home!*
Àlùfẹ́,*turn around and go back home!*
Àlùfẹ́,*turn around and go back home!*

She said, "Well, well, well, even if you do bark, '*gbágà*,' even if you cry, '*wòọ̀òn*,' or make any other noise no one has ever heard before, I'm going with you today, and that's that. My mind's made up, you must understand that." So he said, "Okay," and they continued on.

After they had walked a short distance, he said, "Friend, please, may Ọlọ́'run prevent us from running into trouble," and he carried on in that vein. "When I left home this morning, I hadn't planned to bring a wife to the house. When we get home, I'll have to tell my father and mother to come back with us to pay your bride price. I hadn't told them anything like that when I left; I was only going to the market to buy something." "Yes, but if you go to the market and see something you like, you consider yourself even more fortunate if it turns out to be a new wife. Isn't it all the same thing? You said you had no wife, didn't you?" "Yes, I've never married before." "Please, then, let me go with you to your house. You've already spoken to my parents and it's all settled." Well! Oh, my!

Now listen. The young man stared up in the sky a while longer. Yes, he was really stuck. They carried on for two more hours, and then the man looked up again, and started to sing:

Àlùfẹ́, *turn around and go back home!*
          Àlùfẹ́!
Àlùfẹ́, *turn around and go back home!*
          Àlùfẹ́!
I'll scramble up a tree and then jump to another,
          Àlùfẹ́!
When I've jumped to the tree, I'll then jump to a palm,

Àlùfẹ́!
And when I've jumped to the palm, I'll jump on a rock,
Àlùfẹ́!
Then I'll scamper up and down and shit as I climb,
Àlùfẹ́!
I'll scamper with eyes staring white straight ahead,
Àlùfẹ́!
I'll scamper some more and bark, "gbógì,"
Àlùfẹ́!
When I've barked, "gbógì," next I'll bark, "gbágà,"
Àlùfẹ́!
Àlùfẹ́, turn around and go back home!
Àlùfẹ́!
Àlùfẹ́, turn around and go back home!

Well, the girl insisted he was only trying to frighten her. "Carry on, whether you humiliate your bride or not, even if you cry, 'gbágà,' we're going to your house today. It's decided, I'm going home with you, whether you bark at me or not, it makes absolutely no difference to me. So, let's move on."

Oh, my! You see, the handsome man wasn't human at all! In fact, he was a monkey! He had changed himself into a person just to go to market. And now, ògìrìtówò melon, who had lent him his seeds for teeth, and tòtó plant, who had lent him his smooth, brown skin, were quite nearby. Ha! Oh, no! The girl followed doggedly behind. What would he do? What could he do?

As they got nearer and nearer to the melon, who was waiting to claim his teeth, the monkey-man said, "Friend, please go back home, have pity on me, go back home." "Never!" she said. Well! Huh! He said, "Go back home. Don't become involved in my strange habits. Listen, you!!" "Even if you're a supernatural being and perform marvelous tricks, I'm still going along with you." Oh, dear! Well, so they continued, and on the way he sang again:

Àlùfẹ́, *turn around and go back home!*
   Àlùfẹ́!
Àlùfẹ́, *turn around and go back home!*
   Àlùfẹ́!
I'll scramble up a tree and then jump to another,
   Àlùfẹ́!
And when I've jumped to the palm, I'll jump on a rock,
   Àlùfẹ́!
When I've jumped to the tree, I'll then jump to a palm,
   Àlùfẹ́!
Then I'll scamper up and down and shit as I climb,
   Àlùfẹ́!
I'll scamper with eyes staring white straight ahead,
   Àlùfẹ́!
I'll scamper some more and bark, "gbógì,"
   Àlùfẹ́!
When I've barked, "gbógì," next I'll bark, "gbágà,"
   Àlùfẹ́!
Àlùfẹ́, *turn around and go back home!*
   Àlùfẹ́!
Àlùfẹ́, *turn around and go back home!*

Oh dear, *Olódùmarè*, don't let my mouth kill me. I hope it isn't swelling your cheek? Friends, I'm "The One Who Tells the Story Without Muffing the Job, Son of He with a Slender Neck!" Welcome.

   Okay. Friends, you see, when he reached *ògìrìtówò* melon, he took hold of each of his teeth, snapped them out, and handed them all back. Then he took his own sharp, pointed teeth and fit them into his mouth. The girl said, "Well, even though you've put those awful things in your mouth, I'm marrying you anyway." "Go, back," he said, "get away from here. Go back home and I'll come to meet you there. Go back!" "No," she said, "I won't go back." Well, then they got to *tòtó*, who had given him his skin, and he started to sing again:

Àlùfẹ́, *turn around and go back home!*
    Àlùfẹ́!
Àlùfẹ́, *turn around and go back home!*
    Àlùfẹ́!
I'll scramble up a tree and then jump to another,
    Àlùfẹ́!
And when I've jumped to the palm, I'll jump on a rock,
    Àlùfẹ́!
When I've jumped to the tree, I'll then jump to a palm,
    Àlùfẹ́!
Then I'll scamper up and down and shit as I climb,
    Àlùfẹ́!
I'll scamper with eyes staring white straight ahead,
    Àlùfẹ́!
I'll scamper some more and bark, "gbógì,"
    Àlùfẹ́!
When I've barked, "gbógì," next I'll bark, "gbágà,"
    Àlùfẹ́!
Àlùfé, *turn around and go back home!*
    Àlùfẹ́!
Àlùfẹ́, *turn around and go back home!*

When they reached *tòtó,* the man pulled off his skin in a flash, and handed it back. Then he bent down, took his own skin, and threw it over his shoulders. As soon as his wife saw his thick, shining coat—as if it had come from *Ogún* himself—Ha! "Even though you've performed a miracle like this and covered your whole body with hair," she said, "I'm marrying you anyway." May Ọlọ́'run not let us put our heads in the pathway of death. Amen.

She had no idea what trouble was in store for her—a child born in a good house is spoiled so much that she knows nothing about the world. Friends, let no one spoil his child through overindulgence. Friends, *Olódùmarè,* spare us from meeting trouble along the road. Amen.

You see, as they were going along, they came to a huge outcropping. Well, friends, as they drew nearer, the young man turned and looked at her threateningly, saying, "Friend, go back home." She replied, "Hey! What do you think you're doing? Do you really think you can scare me away now? You shouldn't try to get rid of me like that. After all, I'm your wife." Oh, Lord! Ọlọ́run, I hope this isn't swelling your cheek. Friends, as they neared the rock, oh boy! He started to sing:

> Àlùfẹ́, *turn around and go back home!*
> Àlùfẹ́!
> Àlùfẹ́, *turn around and go back home!*
> Àlùfẹ́!
> *I'll scramble up a tree and then jump to another,*
> Àlùfẹ́!
> *And when I've jumped to the palm, I'll jump on a rock,*
> Àlùfẹ́!
> *When I've jumped to the tree, I'll then jump to a palm,*
> Àlùfẹ́!
> *Then I'll scamper up and down and shit as I climb,*
> Àlùfẹ́!
> *I'll scamper with eyes staring white straight ahead,*
> Àlùfẹ́!
> *I'll scamper some more and bark,* "gbógì,"
> Àlùfẹ́!
> *When I've barked,* "gbógì," *next I'll bark,* "gbágà,"
> Àlùfẹ́!
> Àlùfé, *turn around and go back home!*
> Àlùfẹ́!
> Àlùfẹ́, *turn around and go back home!*

Friends, I congratulate myself "He who tells the story without muffing the job, son of the man with a slender neck!"

Okay. Just then àjànàkú jumped up and landed in a tree. You could hear him go, "gbà." Good God! From there he sailed over to the trunk of a palm tree, *hurrump.* Good God! And from there he hopped on to the side of the inselberg, boom! He barked, "gbókùn, gbókùn, gbókùn, gbóhoò hó."

When his wife saw that, she shit in fright. Her excrement was equal to seven lumps of pounded yam. Friends, oh my! His wife turned around and—"Hey! The fire's been burning all this time and all you did was fan it. Where are you running to now? Have you given up already?" Friends, things had gotten very serious. His wife was shaking all over, *mẹ mẹ mẹ mẹ*. Her breasts were bouncing from side to side, *le le le le. Olódùmarè!* She had surely run into trouble. May *Olódùmarè* prevent us from running into trouble. Amen.

She saw her master's big lower jaw crying out, "*Bómù, bómù, bómù, bómù!*" Oh, my! She was in a terrible predicament. Friends, you see he pulled her by the hand up to the top of the rock, one step after another, *kẹ́ẹ́tẹ́ kẹ́ẹ́tẹ́ kẹ́ẹ́tẹ́*. When they were all the way to the top, he ordered her to bend over and take hold of the rock like an animal. Then he jumped on her back and began copulating, just like an animal does with his mate. *Olódùmarè!* Her jaw was knocking against the hard stone, "*gbùú.*" Then he told her to stand up. Some people will try to use a palm leaf to carry guinea fowl eggs. The eye sees only what it wants to.

Now, when he had fucked her again and again and again, she was thoroughly exhausted. She fell down on her chest, breathing in great gasps on top of the rock. Ah! She realized she needed food. *Àjànàkú* went off to the bush to get her some, and—you know the tree called *ọmọdọ́n* with inedible pear-shaped fruits, also known as *ègbúlù*, the tree hunters climb to keep watch for animals, well, friends, he brought her an *ègbúlù* fruit and told her to eat it. Here she was, an *ọbá's* daughter who ate only rice and pounded yam! She said, "Ah! please sir, I don't eat this!" He told her to eat it—and quickly. Oh my, he slapped her until she put it in her mouth and began to crunch, "*gbùú gbùú.*"

Now, to be brief—I hope this isn't making your cheek swell, friends—after enduring three days of this punishment the girl was hardly fatter than a finger. She was nearly dead. On the morning of the third day, a hunter had climbed up the same ọmọdọ́n tree where the monkey went to collect her food. Now, when the monkey arrived for his wife's food, the hunter observed him. Àjànàkú came, collected the fruits, and told the girl to eat them. Oh, no! He slapped her so severely that she could no longer stand. She had fallen down. "Ah," the hunter said to himself, "how extraordinary! Isn't that a woman I see there?" Ha! The monkey was forcing her to eat the fruits and she chewed, "pùrú pùrú," and swallowed them. Then he ordered her to sit on her haunches. Friends, when the hunter saw that, he crept quietly over to a good vantage point and shot the monkey, with a, kèmùuuu! Ha! My God! His body twisted around and he fell down dead.

Friends, the girl took to her heels in a flash and then saw the hunter. She pleaded with him, "Sir, let me be your wife." He replied, "You! You? After you've been raped by an animal? When you were still a woman of promise, I asked you to marry me, but all you did was insult me and say I wasn't good enough for you. Just leave me alone, please."

Friends, she took hold of the hunter's neck, and, to be brief, he carried her back home. When they got there, friends, her father and mother filled the whole house with drink and their whole property with food until they couldn't think of another thing to do. They sacrificed a cow to the hunter's head. But he said, "No, the girl has become repugnant to heaven and earth, I don't want her any more. She has been raped by a monkey and I want nothing to do with her. Maybe she's even become pregnant." He rejected her totally.

So ever since that day, when we give our child advice, she should listen closely to what we have to say. And that was where I got to before coming back.

—AFRICAN FOLKLORE

How Tsaile Found a Husband

Tsaile was the daughter of a rich *kaptein* (chief). She led the life of a princess and had so many servants that she literally never moved a finger. The daughters of other men went to work in the fields, to hoe and harvest, to milk and to churn, to make pots and bake bread, to fetch water and firewood, but Tsaile had maids for all that. She even had an old woman to feed her porridge as if she were still a baby. Tsaile was perhaps a spoiled girl, but she was exceptional also in another way: She did not sleep on a mat like normal people but could make herself small and creep into an ostrich eggshell. There she slept quite comfortably, thank you. Of course she always slept late, as nobody bothered to wake her, for she had no duties, nothing to do all day but sit and have her hair plaited by the old woman. But all things come to an end, good things as well as bad things. The day came when Tsaile woke up early and felt like getting up. She emerged from her eggshell and made herself big again, like a normal girl. She went out and found the old woman, who was on her way to fetch millet from the grainstore. "Grind corn for me. I want some porridge," ordered the girl. The old woman was suddenly tired of her; she felt old, and it may just happen in life that we feel we have never really liked our job. So she blurted out, "You lazy girl! It is about time you got married. Your husband would teach you that a woman has to work. I am old and you don't leave me time to eat. I am getting lean and sick! Don't you see that your age-mates are all married? For how long will you go on living like a child?"

Tsaile was speechless. Never in her life had anybody contradicted her. She felt hurt and suddenly lonely, as if with the old woman everyone had deserted her. While the old woman went into the grainstore, Tsaile ran away. Yes, just like that, she ran and ran (and remember she had never run before, since she was always carried around on all her journeys). She slowed down a little and walked for a long time. Toward nightfall she came to a lonely hut that had been built by somebody in the middle of the savanna. She looked around but saw nobody, so finally she plucked up courage and went inside the hut. There was no one there, but as soon as she was inside, the voice of an invisible man spoke to her: "Welcome, sweet girl, we are very happy you have come. There is a place to sleep for you here, come and eat first. Then just lie down and rest. Don't be afraid, for to us you are like a sister!"

Tsaile saw a new sleeping mat lying on the floor, and a pot of steaming porridge was waiting there invitingly for her. She was so hungry that she ate without a word and so tired that she lay down and fell asleep at once without thinking how afraid she really was.

The next morning when she got up, there was a pot of fresh porridge waiting for her. When she had finished it and was making ready to set off, she suddenly saw her new sleeping mat rolling itself up and rising in the air. A friendly voice said, "Come with me, I will guide you part of the way to your future home. I will carry your sleeping mat for you. Just follow me." And there she saw the sleeping mat traveling away in front of her through the air. She followed it, but she could not see the person, the owner of the voice who was carrying it. They, that is, she, the mat and the amicable voice, traveled for a long time until they came to a river. "Here I must take my leave," said the voice, "This is the first river you have to cross. Its water contains red ochre, clay of a fine color, just right for a young lady like you. Rub your body with it as much as you like, then travel straight on until you come to the next river, where you may bathe freely. It does not contain water but oil, which is the best to bathe in for young girls like you. It will make you appear healthy and strong. From there you just travel straight on till you come to the third river, which is the most blessed of all the rivers in my land. It contains neither water nor oil but milk, good, fat, sweet, thick milk from which you may drink as much as you like. It will bring you luck." At that moment Tsaile felt a hand on her shoulder, and the mat was placed on her head so that she could carry it along, for in Africa many people prefer transporting their luggage that way, on their heads, which is very convenient since they have strong heads and proud necks. Suddenly she felt she was alone as the voice moved away. She waded into the river and smeared the red clay all over her skin so that she shone like a sunset. Feeling beautiful, she walked on till she came to the oil river. She had never seen so much *mahura* (body oil) in her life.

She rubbed it all over her shiny brown body until she looked like a chestnut. She traveled straight on, feeling much refreshed but hungry, until she saw a white sheen on the horizon. When she came closer, she discovered it was the milk river. She waded through it, until it came up to her lips. She opened her mouth and drank the delicious milk until she was quite satisfied. From there she walked up a path till she came to a town with many big houses, which, however, were all deserted. She walked around all the streets but found no one, not a goat or a chicken. At last she came upon a large house, which she decided must belong to the chief. There at least she could see traces of life. There was one bed and a small cot that had recently been slept in. But the house was terribly dirty, the pots were empty and the whole place looked badly neglected. She could see that no woman's hand had been at work here for a long time. She took a large jar and went down to the well to fetch water. Then she found the grainstore, filled a pot with millet and put it in the mortar to grind it. She could see the mortar had not been used for a long time, and the cooking pots had not been properly washed. She took them down to the well to wash them, then cooked porridge from the millet grains. She made the beds, swept the yard, cleaned the whole house, inside and outside. She, Tsaile, who had never wielded a broom in her life, who had never cleaned a pot, now worked like a maidservant. Why? Was it perhaps the milk river that had worked a miracle on her? Or was it the owner of the mysterious voice who had put a beneficial spell on her? Or was it simply the fact that here there was not a soul to do the work that needed doing so much? When she was ready with her work, the sun was setting and Tsaile expected the owner of the house to come home soon. She did not know to what sort of beings he belonged, for she had heard so many stories of strange, empty towns where all the inhabitants had been eaten by a giant or a witch. To be quite safe, she made herself small and hid in one of the empty pots, which had a crack so that she could see without being seen. No sooner had she stepped into the pot than she heard footsteps and there appeared a tall man, who was very handsome except that he looked sad and despondent. On his back he carried a baby in a cuddle-skin, as if he were a woman. He put down a hoe he was holding, and this astonished Tsaile even more, since hoeing is woman's work in most parts of Africa. He then evidently wanted to put a pot on the fire to cook his meal, when he found to his glad surprise that the fire was lit and the porridge cooked. He looked around for any sign of the good genius who had done all this for him and his baby son, but Tsaile was too small and too well hidden to be discovered by a busy man at nightfall. He fed the child, ate some of the porridge himself, then went to sleep on the well-made bed, after having put the child in his cot. The next morning the child woke up first, hungry. The man got up, fed it some porridge, ate the remainder himself, then tied the baby on his back, took his hoe, and went out to the fields. Only then did Tsaile emerge from her sleeping place—after all she was used to sleeping in a confined space. She cleaned the house again, chopped wood for the fire, fetched water, ground millet, made porridge, swept the yard, made the beds, scrubbed the pots, and so forth. That night the man who behaved as if he were a woman came back to a clean house as if the ghost of his wife had returned to work for him. For he was a widower, this man, whose wife had died and left him alone to look after their only son. Losing her made him so sad and morose that he ceased speaking to people and walked about like one who had died, lonely like a person from another world, he who was once a chief. Now his people had deserted him as one after another they left the town with their families to live somewhere else while the great chief became a shadow of himself. People do not like to live with a chief whose thoughts are always on the graveyard. At last the town was deserted. Some people had moved far away, others not so far, but none wanted to live with the sad chief, so he had to carry his own child on his back, and had to be father and mother at the same time. It was hard work for a man, hoeing and harvesting but he had nothing else to do now that his people no longer came to him for counsel and consultation.

And now some good genius had come to help him in his need. One day, while he was in the fields, he suddenly decided to go home early. He tied his little son on his back and went home. He approached his house from behind, walking softly between the other houses so that he could not be seen or heard. Then suddenly he turned a corner and saw the one who had made his bed and cooked his meals: a girl more beautiful than he had ever seen in his life. He looked at her, then she came up to him and said, "Let me carry your child, I will look after him from now on." And she took the child and tied it on her own back. Tsaile, who had never yet touched a baby and had never had to carry anything in her life, carried on her back another man's child.

She said, "Come inside, the fire is burning, it is cold outside here in the hills, and the hot porridge will do you good." He, the once-powerful chief whom grief had broken, was speechless to find such a wonderful woman working for him and his child. He was deeply relieved that his life's problem created by the loss of his wife was solved for him by...by the owner of the mysterious voice? Tsaile was telling him about her invisible host who had given her the sleeping mat and predicted her future happiness. And while she was talking to him, she served him his meal, and fed the baby, she, Tsaile who had never served anybody and had always been fed like a baby herself, and she who had never worked for others or even for herself now felt so good that she started humming a song. She began a little dance while the chief built and lit a huge fire: He followed her in the dance, and in the song too. You see, in Africa people do this and no one thinks anything of it: making a song and singing it, so that others can pick it up if they are in a like mood, and inventing a new dance to suit the song, while friends and others, if the spirit moves them, may join in when they like. That was exactly what happened: some of the chief's onetime friends lived not too far away in the valley to hear the singing. They saw the fire and said to each other, "Some people have fun up there. We must not miss it!" They went together, some bringing their drums and even a *tumo* and a *lesiba*, the two stringed instruments of South Africa. No need to say that it became a big party as some fetched more wood for the fire, and others fetched beer, for dancing makes you thirsty. Now even those who had settled far away could see the fire and hear the singing and the music. They, too, joined and...stayed. They all reoccupied their old houses, for their chief had become his old self again.

—SOUTH AFRICA

Reverend
Clarence Davis's
(United Methodist Church, Baltimore)
Top Five Most
Romantic
Churches in the
Country:

5. Ben Hill United Methodist in Atlanta

4. John Wesley United Church in Baltimore

3. Riverside Church in New York

2. Abyssinian Baptist Church in Harlem

1. Metropolitan Baptist Church in Washington, D.C.

Gris-gris (for a successful marriage): Join the hands of two dolls with a ribbon. Take some sand and pile it up in a mound. On top of this place nine wax candles, sprinkle the whole with champagne, saying, "Saint Joseph, make this marriage and I'll pay." When the marriage takes place, put a plate of macaroni sprinkled with parsley near a tree in Congo Square in payment.

—LOUISIANA FOLK BELIEF

KEEPING LOVE ALIVE

OTHER THAN FACING down death itself, there is probably no greater challenge in life than keeping love alive. Even with the most compatible partners, there are constant adjustments to be made over time. The couple as a unit changes, the individuals within that unit change, and the times and circumstances in which the couple live change. The couple must respond to all these changes, and the best way to do that is to keep the lines of communication open.

But that is also the most difficult task, because people have a natural tendency to ignore what they think they already know. So the trick is to keep rediscovering your partner. Do not take him or her for granted. Seduction is a key word here. Pay attention to your partner as if you are still seducing him or her. Stay alert to nuance and inference. Don't be afraid to try new things, to experiment, to be silly. Don't be overly judgmental. Be respectful, considerate, and willing to sacrifice sometimes. But never be a resentful martyr. In this chapter I included voodoo practices that are reputed to keep love's flame eternal and folk beliefs about keeping love alive. I've included testimonials about how to recognize when your love life is flagging and ways to spark it up. I've included ruminations about what went wrong with a previous affair or marriage, and how people have applied lessons from those failures to create a stronger, more lasting union.

Ten Ways to Keep Love Alive

1. Say "I love you" at least once a day
2. Surprise your partner 3. Look at difficulties as learning experiences 4. Candlelight—everywhere 5. Exercise together 6. Read poetry or romantic or humorous sections of novels to each other 7. Take turns giving head-to-toe massages 8. Dance in your living room 9. Trust and be trustworthy 10. Set aside private time for just the two of you, without kids, the phone, the TV

SEDUCTION

one day
you gonna walk in this house
and i'm gonna have on a long African
gown
you'll sit down and say "The Black..."
and i'm gonna take one arm out
then you—not noticing me at all—will say "What about
this brother..."
and i'm going to be slipping it over my head
and you'll rapp on about "The revolution..."
while i rest your hand against my stomach
you'll go on—as you always do—saying
"I just can't dig..."
while i'm moving your hand up and down
and i'll be taking your dashiki off
then you'll say "What we really need..."
and i'll be licking your arm
and "The way I see it we ought to..."
and unbuckling your pants
"And what about the situation..."
and taking your shorts off
then you'll notice
your state of undress
and knowing you you'll just say
"Nikki,
isn't this counterrevolutionary...?"

—NIKKI GIOVANNI

BEST PLACES

to go for breakfast in New York, after a night of lovemaking:

- Buppies
- Wilson's
- Sarabeth's Kitchen
- The Canadian Pancake House
- Birdland (for Sunday brunch)
- Windows on the World

—STEPHAN DWECK, ATTORNEY

"THE APPEAL OF
BARRY WHITE'S MUSIC
IS SENSUAL. IT'S DIFFERENT,
IT'S SEXY, IT'S AGGRESSIVE,
IT'S SENSITIVE."

—BARRY WHITE, ABOUT HIMSELF

"'IS IT STILL GOOD TO YA'
KEEPS ME ON TOP OF THE
SITUATION. IT KEEPS ME
ASKING, INQUIRING,
AS OPPOSED TO ACCEPTING,
ASSUMING THINGS."

—NICK ASHFORD

"There was a time I had abandoned the idea of seducing my wife, and she had abandoned the idea of seducing me as well. This happens to many couples: They come to a time when there is a general flatness in bed. We noticed that we had arrived at that stage and decided to kick our sexual relationship into a different gear. We recalled the fun we had when we first met, when sex with each other was not taken for granted. We again began to put energy into setting up dates—gondola rides in the park, Rollerblading by the river in late August, that special hotel with the crackling fire in the lobby during winter. We leave sexy/sensual notes for each other around the house and in unexpected places. Recently I got to the office and opened my briefcase to find a pair of my wife's panties and an explicit suggestion for a lunchtime rendezvous. We explore each other's bodies the way we once did. We don't assume that we know what the other wants. We experiment. We get creative. We nibble, nip, and touch in the same way in different places, and in different ways in the same places. Now, I'm not a believer that constant sex saves a marriage. But I do believe it spices a marriage and can help it keep going."

—CRAIG H., AGE FORTY-TWO, WRITER, DENVER

Hair from your lover's head placed under the band of your hat, worn in your purse, or in your pocket nearest your heart, buried under your lover's doorstep, or nailed to a tree or post, will make that person love you; but, inserted in a green tree, it will run the owner crazy.

The bow from your sweetheart's hat is equally effective in love affairs, worn in your shoe or in your stocking (if you lose it, he will beat you to death), tied around your leg, or thrown into running water (if thrown into stagnant water, he will go crazy). Else you may write a note and slip it in the hatband of the desired person.

— LOUISIANA VOODOO PRACTICE

"IF you find yourself doing bills in the nude and your mate just walks on by, then it's time to put a little mystery back into your relationship.

"Try first making yourself presentable. My husband and I have this rule that we wear around the house what we'd wear if we had guests staying overnight, which means doing our bills in robe and pajamas. Women should remember not to let your man know each and every one of your little beauty secrets. Men ought to keep their belching and farting to a minimum. To some people these suggestions might seem like hardships, things that insulate a married couple from each other's "true" selves. But my husband and I look at it like this: There are no bone-hard rules, just general guidelines by which we try to abide. Besides, putting a little effort into your marriage helps keep it special. Remember, marriage is a date that will last the rest of your lives."

—TIFFANY S., AGE THIRTY, SALES CLERK, SAN DIEGO

"One of the most romantic tables at Jezebel

is the one with the swing near the piano, just to the right of the front door," says Alberta Wright, owner of the Manhattan restaurant. The swing is part of the legacy of Wright's former profession as an antiques dealer. She couldn't part with her cherished possessions, so she brought them with her to her restaurant. Diaphanous shawls hang from every ceiling pipe; more than a dozen antique chandeliers glitter in the night; iron patio chairs surround tables with colorful mismatched cloths, and candles flicker in the shadows. Palms and assorted foliage tower overhead and a jazz pianist shows up nightly to entertain the diners.

Wright comes from South Carolina. Though her mother never formally taught her to cook, Wright learned by watching. But as an eighteen-year-old mother living in New York City, she began cooking in earnest. Her first meals were those she remembered her mother making, and they were spicy. "In the South, we used lots of pepper because we grew pepper," she explained. In this recipe, Wright has given us a dish to spice up any romance.

JEZEBEL'S SPICY HONEY CHICKEN FOR TWO

½ chicken, seasoned to taste with salt and West African pepper
½ cup (1 stick) unsalted butter
½ onion, chopped medium fine
½ teaspoon garlic
1 tablespoon ginger, chopped fine
½ teaspoon cinnamon
1 teaspoon flour
2 tablespoons honey
1 cup water

1. In an 8-inch iron skillet over a medium flame, sauté chicken in butter until browned on both sides and half-cooked.
2. Remove chicken from skillet. Keep butter over flame and add onion, garlic, ginger, and cinnamon, stirring constantly. When golden to dark brown, add flour. When flour is mixed in well, stir in honey and water. Return chicken to skillet with sauce and cook for about 20 minutes.

Marrow of My Bone

Fondle me
caress
and cradle
me
with your lips
withdraw
the nectar from
me
teach me there
is
someone

—Mari Evans

FOOD is the life's blood

of love. If you hadn't noticed it through your personal experiences—the effect of having someone prepare an extra-special meal, taking someone to an especially good restaurant, feeding your partner, or letting your partner sip from your wine glass—then you can pick it up from the many references in literature. Below is a romantic Afro-centric meal from my Kwanzaa cookbook.

Cut the recipes in half for a romantic meal à deux, or prepare for a group or your favorite friends—lovers, married couples, or singles looking for romance.

MENU

Tanzanian Fruit and Cashew Salad with Rum Cream

Grandma's Creamed Cornbread

New-Fashioned Fried Chicken

Passion Fruit Mousse with Tropical Fruits

TANZANIAN FRUIT AND CASHEW SALAD WITH RUM CREAM

Could this salad have been the forefather of Ambrosia? Make it well ahead of serving, since it only gets better as the fruit macerates in the rum cream. Here's how to choose a ripe pineapple: It should "give" slightly when squeezed and should smell sweet. The rind should have a golden cast, and a leaf should pull out easily with a gentle tug.

SERVES 6 TO 8

One large ripe pineapple
½ cup heavy (whipping) cream
¼ cup dark rum
2 tablespoons honey
2 tangerines, peeled and sectioned
½ cup cashews, for garnish (about 2 ounces)
¼ cup shredded fresh coconut (or sweetened coconut flakes), for garnish

1. Using a large sharp knife, cut away the crown of leaves and the pineapple rind. If desired, remove the ``eyes'' with the tip of the knife. Quarter the pineapple, then remove the tough core from each quarter. Cut the pineapple into 1-inch pieces, and transfer them to a medium bowl.

2. In a small bowl, whisk together the cream, rum, and honey. Stir this into the pineapple. Cover, and refrigerate until well chilled, at least 2 hours or overnight.

3. Fold the tangerines into the pineapple mixture.

4. If the cashews are salted, place them in a sieve and rinse under cold running water to remove the salt; pat dry with paper towels. Chop the cashews coarsely. Sprinkle the top of the salad with the chopped cashews and the coconut, and serve.

GRANDMA'S CREAMED CORNBREAD

You'd have to go a long mile to find a cakier, more finely textured cornbread than this one. The creamed corn has something to do with it, of course.

MAKES ONE 9-INCH ROUND CORNBREAD

4 tablespoons (½ stick) unsalted butter, melted
1 cup yellow cornmeal, preferably stone-ground
¾ cup all-purpose flour
2 tablespoons granulated sugar
1 tablespoon plus 1 teaspoon baking powder
½ teaspoon salt
One 8-ounce can creamed corn
1 cup milk
1 large egg, well beaten

1. Preheat the oven to 450°F.
2. Pour 2 tablespoons of the melted butter into a 9-inch cake pan, and bake for 5 minutes, until the cake pan is very hot.
3. Meanwhile, in a medium bowl, whisk together the cornmeal, flour, sugar, baking powder, and salt. Make a well in the center of this mixture, and pour the creamed corn, milk, remaining 2 tablespoons butter, and egg into the well. Stir until smooth. Pour the batter into the hot cake pan.
4. Bake until the cornbread is golden brown and a toothpick inserted in the center comes out clean, 30 to 35 minutes. Remove the cornbread from the oven, and let it stand for 15 minutes before serving.

NEW-FASHIONED FRIED CHICKEN

The old-fashioned classic fried chicken used rendered lard, something not found in a lot of households these days. Olive oil works very well, especially with high-powered seasonings. Here are a couple of hints for perfecting your fried-chicken technique:

• Try to use a heavy skillet, such as well-seasoned cast iron, in order to hold the oil's heat and prevent the chicken crust from burning on the bottom.

• Be sure to use enough oil to reach halfway up the sides of the skillet, and heat the oil until it is very, very hot—but not smoking. This will ensure a crisp coating and discourage the chicken from becoming greasy.

• Be sure the oil is hot before you dredge the chicken in the seasoned flour. If the flour sits too long on the chicken, it will become gummy and the coating will be substandard.

• White meat cooks faster than dark meat. So that everything will be finished at the same time, give the dark meat a head start by frying it for about 7 minutes before adding the breasts.

• Fresh chicken is far superior to frozen. If the bones are black inside after cooking, your butcher is using frozen chickens.

SERVES 3 OR 4

1½ cups vegetable oil
1½ cups olive oil
One 3¾-pound chicken, cut into 8 pieces
2 tablespoons Old Bay Seasoning
2 teaspoons hot pepper sauce, or to taste
2 cups all-purpose flour
2 teaspoons poultry seasoning
1 teaspoon paprika
1 teaspoon freshly ground black pepper
¾ teaspoon salt

1. In a large, heavy skillet, heat the vegetable and olive oils over medium-high heat until very hot but not smoking.

2. Meanwhile, in a large bowl, combine the Old Bay Seasoning with the hot pepper sauce and toss the chicken well to coat it with the seasoning.

3. Place the flour, poultry seasoning, paprika, pepper, and salt in a heavy paper grocery bag. A couple of pieces at a time, shake the dark meat in the seasoned flour and place in the hot oil. Cook, turning once, for 7 minutes. (Adjust the heat so that the oil stays hot but doesn't begin to smoke.)

4. Shake the breast pieces in the seasoned flour, and add them to the oil. Cook all the chicken together for 5 minutes, turning once. Cover the skillet tightly, reduce the heat to medium-low, and cook for 15 minutes. Remove the cover and cook, turning occasionally, until the chicken is deeply browned and shows no sign of pink at the bone when prodded with the tip of a sharp knife.

5. Using kitchen tongs (not a meat fork, which will pierce the juicy chicken), transfer the chicken pieces to a paper bag or paper towels to drain. Serve the chicken hot, warm, or at room temperature.

PASSION FRUIT MOUSSE WITH TROPICAL FRUITS

SERVES 8

20 ripe passion fruits (see note)
6 large eggs, separated, at room temperature
1¾ cups granulated sugar
2 tablespoons cornstarch
Grated zest of 1 large lemon
2 packages plain unflavored gelatin
6 tablespoons cold water
1 ripe papaya, peeled, seeded, and cut into ½-inch-thick slices
1 ripe mango, pitted, peeled, and cut into ½-inch-thick slices
2 ripe kiwis, peeled and cut crosswise into ¼-inch-thick rounds
1 medium banana, peeled and cut into ¼-inch-thick rounds
Grated zest and juice of 1 medium lime

1. Using a serrated knife, cut the passion fruits in half crosswise. Using a dessertspoon, scoop the yellow pulp and seeds out of the shells and place them in a fine sieve set over a medium bowl.

2. Using a wooden spoon, rub the pulp in the sieve to extract the juices; discard the seeds in the sieve. You should have ¾ cup plus 2 tablespoons juice.

3. In the top part of a double boiler, whisk the egg yolks with 1½ cups of the sugar until thick and pale yellow, about 2 minutes. Whisk in the passion fruit juice and cornstarch.

4. Cook the juice mixture over simmering water, stirring constantly with a wooden spoon, until a thermometer inserted in the mixture reads 175°F and it lightly coats the spoon, 8 to 10 minutes. Stir in the lemon zest. Remove the top of the double boiler from the heat.

5. In a small bowl, sprinkle the gelatin over the cold water; let it stand for 5 minutes. Then place the bowl in a small saucepan of simmering water, and stir constantly until the gelatin has dissolved, about 2 minutes. Whisk the gelatin into the passion fruit mixture. Refrigerate, whisking occasionally, until the mixture is cool and beginning to set, about 15 minutes.

6. In a large grease-free bowl, using a hand-held electric mixer set at low speed, beat the egg whites until foamy. Increase the speed to high and beat just

until the whites form soft peaks. Gradually beat in the remaining ¼ cup sugar, beating just until the whites form stiff, shiny peaks. Stir about one fourth of the beaten whites into the passion fruit mixture. Then gently fold in the remaining whites.

7. Lightly grease a 2-quart fluted mold. Pour in the passion fruit mousse and smooth the top. Cover tightly with aluminum foil, and refrigerate until firm, at least 6 hours or overnight.

8. In a large bowl, combine the papaya, mango, kiwis, banana, lime zest, and lime juice. Cover tightly with plastic wrap and refrigerate until ready to serve, up to 1 day.

9. To unmold the mousse, wet a clean kitchen towel with hot water and wring it out. Invert the mold onto a serving platter and wrap the hot, moist towel around the mold; let it stand for 30 seconds, and then remove the towel. Hold the mold and the platter together and shake firmly once or twice to unmold the mousse. Remove the mold.

10. Surround the mousse with the tropical fruits. Cut the mousse into wedges, and garnish each serving with a spoonful of the fruit.

N O T E : You may substitute ¾ cup bottled passion fruit juice (available at health food stores) plus 2 tablespoons passion fruit liqueur (such as La Grande Passion) for the ripe passion fruit juice. Use only 1 cup sugar in step 3.

TO KEEP A LOVER FAITHFUL: WRITE HIS NAME ON A PIECE OF PAPER AND PUT IT UP THE CHIMNEY. PRAY TO IT THREE TIMES A DAY.

—LOUISIANA FOLK BELIEF

"**Not** long after our marriage, my husband abandoned me both emotionally and physically. After years of this, I finally demanded a divorce, which should not have come as a surprise to him, seeing that I had been warning him about it for most of our marriage. Nonetheless he seemed caught off guard. He actually cried. I reminded him that I had warned him many times. I had communicated, he just hadn't listened.

"In the wake of the divorce, however, I see that I was a poor communicator, for in telling him of my physical and emotional needs, I didn't recognize what he was putting into the marriage, which was a paycheck to make the material dreams of our marriage come true, and enduring insult and stress to do it. I sometimes actually denigrated his contributions. I would say, 'Money is not all there is to a marriage,' or 'The house, money, and job don't matter if there is no relationship. No emotional bond.' I should have said, 'I appreciate all you do for us. I appreciate your sacrifices and recognize your achievements. But there are many sides to a marriage and they are equally important.' That, I think, would have been communicating without belittling him, communicating without reproach. I think, if I had taken that tack, he actually would have heard me."

—SHARON R., AGE THIRTY-EIGHT, PERSONAL TRAINER, ATLANTA

"THERE IS NO SECRET
TO A LONG MARRIAGE—
IT'S HARD WORK.
...IT'S SERIOUS BUSINESS,
AND CERTAINLY NOT
FOR COWARDS."

—OSSIE DAVIS

If you get a love letter from your boyfriend, lay it open and then fold the letter in nine different ways and pin it on your clothes, right over your heart. Let it stay there until you go to bed. Then put the letter in your left glove, placing the glove under your head. If your lover is true to you, you will dream of gold or diamonds, but if you dream you see washing or graves, you will either lose him by death or go through poverty for a long time. —LOUISIANA FOLK BELIEF

"I'M NOT A MILLIONAIRE.

Probably never will be. And for years this fact prevented me from getting my wife gifts. A birthday would come and go, Valentine's Day, and anniversaries, but I was embarrassed at not being able to buy her the two dozen long-stemmed roses my heart told me she deserved; I was embarrassed, after six years, at not being able to give her a pair of big diamond earrings to go with the teeny, tiny diamond of her wedding ring.

"But the evening before the eighth anniversary of our first meeting, I was taking the bus home when this woman boarded. She was thirty-five-ish, attractive in a kind of raw way, and boozed up. She immediately set her sights on seducing the teenager sitting behind me, and in her seduction I heard her whine about her boyfriend, how, after years of a relationship, he never gave her anything. 'Not even a card on my birthday,' she said, 'Not even a couple of lousy flowers from the Korean grocer. It doesn't have to be expensive.' That night I handmade a note card for my wife on the occasion of the eighth anniversary of our meeting. A few days later I bought some inexpensive flowers for her. Once, when she complained about an especially stressful work week, I simply drew her a bubble bath to help her relax. That chance meeting on the bus made me realize that it *is* the thought and the attention that counts. And thank God, I learned it before it was too late."

—JIM G., THIRTY-SIX, PUBLIC RELATIONS REPRESENTATIVE, MIAMI

See the Heart

Those who have ceased to love
Have not ceased to need,
Those who have ceased to care
Have not ceased to bleed;
Do not weigh the words that
Never ask, the minds that never
Seek, nor mark the averted faces,
But see the heart.

—Jean Toomer

IF
YOU SWEEP SOMEONE'S FEET, HE WILL RUN OFF.

—African-American
folk belief

The box above the stage is the most romantic seat at the Apollo Theater in Harlem. There's just something about being in the same seats that once housed James Brown and Diahann Carroll. You get a real feel for African-American history and entertainment.

Romance can take place practically anywhere. The usual locales are cafés, concerts, or plays. But the best places to be romantic in the truest sense are where we can reflect on what we have gone through as a people. In that reflection we can find the strength to make a commitment to a strong black union. And as we all know, a strong black union equals a strong black future. Busch Gardens in Tampa, Florida, with its African theme park, is one such place. On the more serious—yet still entertaining—side you can focus on the market-places and scenes of African village life. Or you can look and laugh at the spectacle of the hundreds of African fauna that spans the park's many acres. There is even a replica of the Congo River rapids.

Busch Gardens
3000 East Busch Boulevard and 40th Street
Tampa, FL 33674
(813) 988–5171

If fine art will inspire you and your significant other to hug and snuggle, there is the Museum of African-American Art, also in Tampa. The museum includes more than 130 works of art from painting and sculp-tures from the diaspora and dating from the late 1800s to today. Included are pieces from such luminaries as Romare Bearden and Hale Woodruff.

Museum of African-American Art
1308 North Marion Street
Tampa, FL 33602
(813) 272–2466

Music always gets the romantic juices flowing, and there is no better place for a historical, worldwide perspective on black music than the New Orleans Jazz and Heritage Festival held every year in late April. The festival serves up a rich gumbo of zydeco, jazz, and blues, as well as Afro-Caribbean amalgams.

New Orleans Jazz and Heritage Festival
1205 North Rampat Street, P.O. Box 53407
New Orleans, LA 70153-3407
(504) 522-4786; (800) 535-8747

Every relationship needs spiritual sustenance, whether it springs from church, mosque, synagogue, or temple. The Abyssinian Baptist Church is the largest and one of the best known African-American places of worship in the country. And while the church is Christian, it is of cultural importance to every black American. Its founder, Thomas Paul, was one of the early nineteenth-century black preachers who helped make black churches independent in America. And from Abyssinian's pulpit, Congressman Adam Clayton Powell, Jr., reigned as one of the most influential black men in America. So, regardless of your creed, drop by the church, enjoy the choir and silently renew the spiritual bonds that are the foundation of strength for all couples.

Abyssinian Baptist Church
132 West 138th Street
New York, NY 10030
(212) 862-7474

"When I used to cook, Herbert would always catch my butt in his hands. **It's amazing what a touch can do.** It lets you know, 'I'm here.' **Simple but lovable.** That's what I tell my kids: Keep it simple. **Believe it or not, when Herbert and I wake in the morning, we kiss.** When we're tired, we just rub feet or somethin', we always touch, and that's what we do with our kids, we kiss a lot and we always touch. **You must touch each other."** —Sylvia Woods

"Black men have a remarkable reputation as silver-throated lovers, but when it comes to the daily grind of sustaining a family, we have a reputation for coming up short. That is our rap, and I allowed that rap to haunt my marriage and ultimately destroy it. In the process of trying to support my family—working two, sometimes three jobs—I left my wife wanting for friendship and for physical companionship. My wife would understand, I thought. After all, we shared the same dreams for our family: a good education for the kids, vacations, a decent retirement. So after ten years of working and swallowing indignation and frustration in the workplace, I achieved my goal of financial security. I thought my wife would be there cheering when I crossed the finish line. But when I crossed the finish line, she said *we* were finished. Period.

"I'm happily remarried now and my second marriage works because I learned this lesson: In a marriage the relationship *must* come first. This is not to suggest that you should trim your ambitions because of your marriage. But even in a busy life, make time for each other. A marriage is not a cactus, but a delicate tropical bloom that needs regular nourishment and care to flourish."

—CHARLIE W., AGE FORTY-ONE, FAST FOOD FRANCHISE OWNER, DALLAS

"The capacity to love is so tied to being able to be awake, to being able to move out of yourself and be with someone else in a manner that is not about your desire to possess them, but to be with them, to be in union and communion." —bell hooks

WHEN BREAD OR CAKE OR PIE BURNS IN SPITE OF YOU, YOUR HUSBAND OR LOVER IS ANGRY.

—AFRICAN-AMERICAN FOLK SUPERSTITION

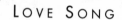

LOVE SONG

I have no sister,
I have no cousin,
I have a wound,
Maria, that is hurting me.

Last evening
When they thought I was dead,
With the light of your eyes
They brought me back to life.

—AFRO-VENEZUALAN

"I WISH that through some premonition I had known that my husband would be coming into my life, and I wish that I had run into him earlier. When I met him, the qualities of what makes a good husband and a good marriage crystallized before my eyes. A married couple must have a similar capacity for, say, love and affection. And, for a good marriage, they should have similar hopes and expectations for the marriage. For instance, both sets of parents were married for over thirty years, until the deaths of our mothers. This is not to say that if one of us had come from a broken household, we couldn't have gotten married, but it is to say that we'd have to look long and hard at our expectations for our marriage and how we intended to meet those expectations. Another thing about my husband is that he is sincerely interested in me and is supportive of me in all my endeavors. There is not an iota of jealousy. He is a constant and reliable source of encouragement."

—CAROL T., AGE THIRTY-EIGHT, ATTORNEY, DENVER

THE MAN WHO TOOK A WATER MOTHER FOR HIS BRIDE

There was a poor country man named Domingos living alone in his cabin not far from the edge of a certain river. He had no family whatever, and as for his garden, it barely produced enough to keep him alive. No matter how he cared for his corn, it did not flourish. Other farmers who lived near Domingos were also poor and wretched, but Domingos was the most unlucky of them all.

One morning Domingos went to his corn to take a few ears to eat. As he went from one stalk to another , he noticed that some of the ears had already been picked, and he wondered who had been heartless enough to take the food from his mouth. The next day he went again to the field and saw that more ears had been picked. Anger swelled in his breast, and he swore to catch the thief and punish him. So that night he took his cane knife and went out and hid in his cornfield at a place where he could see to all sides. He put grass and straw over him so that he would be invisible. He waited while the night grew long and the moon moved across the sky. Sleep was coming over him. His eyes began to close. Then, on the side of the field near the river, there was the rustle of someone walking through the cornstalks. Now he was awake. He clutched his knife, thinking, *I will surely kill the one who is coming to rob me.* He heard the person approaching. He heard the sound of an ear being broken from its stalk. He heard another ear being taken. He saw the shadow of a person. He saw the person, and he left his hiding place and ran forward. What he found surprised him, for the one taking his corn was a water woman who lived with others of her kind in the depths of the river. He seized her, shouting and threatening harm, but he did not strike the water mother. The moon was shining brightly and he saw her beauty. He said, "Why do you steal the food that barely keeps me alive?" She answered, "I was hungry, I meant you no harm." He said, "I should punish you." But she answered, "Let me go. I will return to the river. Henceforth I will go elsewhere for food." Domingos's heart softened. It was warmed by the water woman's voice and her appearance. He said, "Why should I let you go?" She answered, "How would it benefit you to keep me?" And Domingos said, "Why, if I kept you, I would not be alone. I would have a wife like anyone else." She said, "It is not possible. When has a water person ever married with a land person?"

But Domingos was captivated by her voice and her beauty. He asked her to remain. He supplicated her. At last, moved by the warmth of his entreaties, the water woman said, "We have been told by the old people that those who live on land and in the water cannot mix. Once before it happened that a young water woman was taken as a wife by a land person. At first all went well. But after a while the man began to abuse her. He did not treat her as well as in the beginning. And as time passed, he began to ridicule her origins. He said with contempt, 'What can I expect from you, since you are a mere water woman?' And he spoke this way about her among the people of the village. And one night he beat her, saying, 'Water woman! What are you doing living in my house among humans?' She departed from his house then, she returned to the river. The water people said, 'It has always been this way. We must never try to live with the land people.' "

Domingos answered her, saying, "In my eyes you are not a water woman. You are only a woman. What do I care where you come from? Stay here with me, live in my house with me." And so the water woman stayed. She went to his house with him. She became his wife. And because of that, Domingos's fortunes changed. The corn in his field grew large ears. His goats and cattle multiplied. Other people who lived nearby began to praise Domingos for his industry. Whereas once he had been too poor to listen to, now they listened respectfully when he spoke, because he was a man of substance. Domingos built a new house. People came to him for help when they were in need. He had much surplus corn hanging from the branches of the large tree that shaded his roof. But Domingos never stopped to think about where his good fortune came from. He became arrogant. And one evening after he had been drinking to excess, he began to abuse his wife. He said, "Our children are bad-mannered. Why have you set them such a bad example?" He said, "Why is it that while I work hard in the field, you do nothing?" He said, "The people who live nearby, they say bad things about you. Why are you so careless in your ways?" Domingos went on this way, accusing her and abusing her, but she did not reply to him. And her silence angered Domingos still more. He said, "You are a sullen woman. Why don't you speak when you are spoken to?" Still his wife said nothing. And at last Domingos shouted at her, "*Mãe d'agua!* Water woman! You who came out of the river!"

When she heard these words, the water woman arose from where she was sitting. She went out the door of the cabin. Domingos followed her, shouting curses at the water people. But something happened to Domingos. He found that he could not walk, for his feet were rooted to the ground. He saw his wife go toward the river. One by one his children came from the house and followed their mother. When she reached the river's edge, the woman went into the water and disappeared. Her children entered the water and disappeared. Domingos saw his goats and cattle going toward the river. One by one his goats entered the water. One by one his cattle entered the water. They descended. They were seen no more. Domingos cried out. He tried to follow, but he could not move from where he stood. Then he saw the corn ears that hung in his large tree begin to move. One by one the ears moved through the air as though they were flying. They went to the river. They went into the water and disappeared. And after that, Domingos's house and everything that was in it moved toward the river. Domingos called out, "My house! My house!" But the house went forward and entered the river. The fences Domingos had built to hold his cattle departed. The big tree that had shaded his house departed. The palms that grew all around departed. Everything that had belonged to Domingos departed and followed the water woman into the river. Only then did Domingos's feet become uprooted. He went here, he went there, looking for things that had once belonged to him.

Everything was gone. Domingos had nothing. And he lived to the end of his days as the poorest of all men.

—Afro-American Folklore

MAY IS AN UNLUCKY MONTH TO MARRY IN.

—AFRICAN-AMERICAN FOLK
SUPERSTITION

CANARY
for Michael S. Harper

Billie Holiday's burned voice
had as many shadows as lights,
a mournful candelabra against a sleek piano,
the gardenia her signature under that ruined face.

(Now you're cooking, drummer to bass,
magic spoon, magic needle.
Take all day if you have to
with your mirror and your bracelet of song.)

Fact is, the invention of women under siege
has been to sharpen love in the service of myth.

If you can't be free, be a mystery.

—RITA DOVE

"When you marry, you're not just marrying one person, but, to some extent, your spouse's friends and family. And as a loving spouse, you wouldn't want to make your husband or wife give up a meaningful relationship just because that friend or family member gets on your nerves. You learn to compromise. You learn to make accommodations.

"For instance, my best friend grates on my husband's nerves like fingers drawn across a blackboard. I know because he periodically tells me so. And when my husband knows she's coming to visit, he tries to make himself scarce. But recently I was on a business trip and my friend broke her leg in an accident. My husband called me up and told me the news. I was closing a deal at work, and I had wall-to-wall meetings that started early in the morning and went until late at night. There was no time to pick up the phone to order flowers, much less to think about what kind of flowers should be sent or to come up with a thoughtful note.

"After the deal was completed, I called my friend to find out how she was doing, and she thanked me for the flowers and the kind, witty note. It really raised her spirits, she said. At first I thought my secretary had sent the flowers and note, but when she told me she hadn't, I knew it could only be one other person: my funky monkey."

—LORI H., AGE THIRTY-FIVE, REAL ESTATE ATTORNEY, LOS ANGELES

The Greater Trickster

A husband once told his wife that he was a more clever person in high tricks than his father-in-law.

The wife laughed loudly and replied that her husband was not serious. "My father," she said, "had an idea of high tricks long before your mother was born, so you cannot be more clever than he."

The young man argued no longer with his wife. He rather chose to test his father-in-law in order to prove his mettle in high tricks.

One day he sent an empty pot through his wife to the father-in-law, asking him to fill it with the sweetest wine imaginable. The wine, he warned, must neither be native palm wine nor the imported wine. He advised that as soon as the pot was filled, the father-in-law should please inform him.

This young man, of course, thought that it would take his father-in-law a long time to find a solution to this problem of a new wine.

To his great surprise, the young man's father-in-law lost no time, but sent a messenger to let his son-in-law know that the wine in question was ready.

The text of the message sent was: "Your wine is ready. You must send someone who is neither a man nor a woman to carry it to you."

On receipt of this astonishing message from his father-in-law, the young man perceived that it would not become possible for him to have the wine, as there was no such person in the world.

So, his father-in-law, without doubt, was a more clever person in high tricks than he.

Young men think that old men are fools, but old men know that young men are fools.

—EFIK FOLK TALE

"THE LONGER YOU'VE been married, the more flexible you have to be in giving your partner space to grow and develop new interests and new friends. But it is also important to grow together, develop new interests together, meet new people together. That way you are continually sharing experiences, bonding with each other, and this helps maintain a strong, fulfilling marriage. It's not always easy, and sometimes you have to be creative.

"WHEN MY WIFE realized that she was getting older and needed a way to keep the pounds off, she decided to start running. I hate running. It's bad for my knees and I get shin splints. But I realized that I, too, needed a way to burn off excess fat. What to do? I bought a mountain bike and started accompanying my wife on her early-morning runs. And there you'll see us four days a week, up and down the hills of San Francisco together, huffing and puffing and bonding away."

—LEON T., AGE THIRTY-SEVEN, STORE MANAGER, SAN FRANCISCO

The Top Ten
Most Romantic Places
to Watch the Stars

10. Puerta Vallarta, Mexico

9. Any field along the road from Soweto
to Johannesburg in South Africa

8. Atop the Palisades in New Jersey, overlooking
the Hudson River

7. Seventy-ninth Street Boat Basin in Manhattan

6. Near any one of the ice mountains made of
red rock in Sedona, Arizona

5. Zuma Beach, Malibu, California

4. Phosphorescent Bay, La Parguera, Puerto Rico

3. Off the beach on Isla Verde, Puerto Rico

2. The papal palace, Avignon, France

1. The island of Capri

— Gilda Matthews, astrologer

THE WIFE WHO PRACTICED WITCHCRAFT

Once upon a time there was a man who had several wives, and they all bore him children except one. It is not unusual for a young wife to remain barren for the first few years after her marriage, and then later to have children in abundance—the problem is already mentioned in the Bible. Because girls are often married very young in Africa, they needed time to develop into full-grown women. This woman did not, however; she never had a baby, so people began to regard her with contempt at the worst, or at best with polite pity. It is only natural that she should begin to brood, and hatch jealousy against the other wives, who had more babies than they could cope with. Gradually she began to nourish a hatred against nature or the world, for no reaction is more natural in times of misfortune than asking "Why me?"

One day her husband lost a child: one of his fertile wives' children died, and not long afterward the child of another of his wives died. In such circumstances most people in Africa would think of only one cause: witchcraft. The idea of a contagious disease was unknown in Africa, and in any case unacceptable, for whom can you blame if your enemy is invisible? Witchcraft is the cause of suffering, by means of magic. If a woman's child dies, it is the woman who suffers: the child is dead, but the mother goes on grieving and wondering what she did to deserve this. And that is precisely the reason for the belief in witchcraft. Those who suffer from an unjust fate will blame someone who has reasons for jealousy. So the one who is already unhappy is loaded with the gravest possible accusation on top of her misfortune: that of black magic. In Africa the mere suspicion of witchcraft is enough to ostracize a person. What does a man do when he suspects his wife of witchcraft? He will try to find evidence. So this man waited one day until nightfall when everybody had gone to sleep. He then rose from his couch, emerged noiselessly from his hut, and took up a strategic position near the entrance to the cattle kraal, where he could see but not be seen. Near midnight he saw the woman come out of her hut, entirely naked. She went out of the compound without noticing her husband. Having seen this, the husband went to bed. The next morning she was back as if nothing had happened, got up cheerfully, pounded grain, swept the yard, fetched water like all the other women. That night, to make quite sure, the husband took up the same position to spy on his wife. Again he saw her coming out of her hut with no clothes on, leaving the compound. Now there was no doubt left in his mind: This wife was a witch who went out to practice her infernal work in the middle of the night, and her nakedness was proof positive—only witches would go out without clothes on, especially at night. That morning he stood in the courtyard where everyone could hear him, even those who were inside the huts, and he said aloud, "That which is done here at night is dangerous. The person who does dangerous things must go home. She must go home with her dangerous habits and not bring them back here. She has no one to blame but herself if she is not allowed to live in peace here. Let her go to her parents, who will give her advice. Go home now before I club you! Go take your things with you at once. Why are my children dying?"

The woman in question knew, as did everybody in the compound, that the commandment to go was directed at her and at no one else. She packed her meager belongings and left the compound without a word. Those who would like to jeer at her were silenced by their own fear of her witchcraft. That was the only comfort she had in her double bad luck: to be without children and to be expelled by her husband. When she arrived in her parents' home, they questioned her as to why she was sent back, but she pretended not to know or not to understand what she was accused of. Nevertheless her father had his suspicions. He was a good man who liked evil to come out in the open; he was also brave and prepared to face defeat. He went to see his daughter's husband to ask him why he had chased her out. The husband told him, "I saw her in the middle of the night, twice, going out to wherever women go in the middle of the night, and she was as naked as a frog. I do not know where she learned that, but I do not want to keep such a woman in my homestead. I did her no harm, I sent her back and did not club her, though you know I had a right to do so in the circumstances. Now I will claim back the cattle I paid you for your daughter. Two of my children died. While I am still wondering what this dangerous thing is, it has already caught my testicles! Perhaps I should have hit her with my club, but I relied on your righteousness to do justice."

The woman's husband was a chief in his own right, so he could claim his cattle back. Of course such a grave matter had to be investigated by the village council. The elders believed the husband's testimony; they also heard all his wives, one by one. The elders came to the conclusion that there was evidence for the practice of witchcraft, and the poor childless woman was sentenced to death. In those days the death penalty for women of a certain social status was execution by hanging. The woman was taken to a very tall tree in the hills and there she was hanged literally by her own apron strings.

The woman's father was deeply saddened by this cruel loss of his eldest daughter. Instead of returning the cattle he had received for her, he offered his younger daughter as a replacement, hoping to have as yet grandchildren with the chief as their father. The latter did not feel like "nursing another snake from the same nest," but the council of elders ruled in favor of his father-in-law, stating that "There is no need to believe that if there is one rotten fruit on the tree, they should all be bad." So the dead wife's sister moved into the chief's compound to occupy her sister's hut. Unlike the latter, she was a shy and attractive young girl who pleased her husband in spite of his misgivings. She bore him several children, making up for all the sufferings of the past.

—SOUTH AFRICA

TO GET RID OF A RIVAL IN LOVE, PUT HIS NAME IN SOME ASHES AND LET THE CHICKENS PICK IN THE ASHES.

—LOUISIANA FOLK BELIEF

What's the hot drink of the house at the Glam Slam, a club in Miami owned by rock/funk master, formerly known as Prince? The peachy, punchy Woo-Woo! It is made of equal parts vodka and peach schnapps, with a splash of Chambord. And what does it look like? Well, Purple Rain, of course!

"When I first started dating my wife, she was a real party person. She liked entertaining friends at home, going to other people's parties, going out dancing, and hitting after-hours spots. We were perfectly matched. But as time went on, things changed, or rather she did. And while she didn't exactly become a recluse, she certainly became more of a homebody, while I still liked going out and having a good time. We talked about the problem and came up with this solution: We worked out signals— she would pull on her earlobe or earring to indicate that she would like to leave in a half hour or so; she would twist her wedding band to indicate that *we must leave now!* In the year we have been doing this, it has worked great. I get enough partying to keep me happy (although not quite as much as I would like) and she feels good in that she has a way of telling me when she's had enough without attracting attention or embarrassing our host."

—LARRY C., AGE FIFTY, PUBLICIST, MINNEAPOLIS

TO GET REVENGE ON A WOMAN, KEEP A BIT OF HER HAIR, AND ALL HER HAIR WILL FALL OUT.

—LOUISIANA FOLK BELIEF

"A lot of brothers—especially those in their thirties and forties—still feel a hot meal should be waiting for them when they get home from work, even when their wives work too. Today, it is unlikely that a man with those kinds of expectations will have a successful marriage. My wife and I used to eat out a lot. But that got a little expensive, so now we take turns or cook up a mess of stews and casseroles over the weekend. The first one home during the week microwaves that night's meal."

—JON P., AGE FORTY-TWO, LIBRARIAN, ATLANTA

"**D**on't you know you can't git de best of no woman in de talkin' game? Her tongue is all de weapon a woman got," George Thomas chided Gene. "She could have had mo' sense, but she told God no, she'd rather take it out in hips. So God give her her ruthers. She got plenty hips, plenty mouf and no brains."

"Oh, yes, womens is got sense too," Mathilda Moseley jumped in. "But they got too much sense to go 'round braggin' about it like y'all do. De lady people always got de advantage of mens because God fixed it dat way."

"Whut ole black advantage is y'all got?" B. Moseley asked indignantly. "We got all de strength and all de law and all de money and you can't git a thing but whut we jes' take pity on you and give you."

"And dat's jus' de point," said Mathilda triumphantly. "You *do* give it to us, but how come you do it?" And without waiting for an answer Mathilda began to tell why women always take advantage of men:

You see, in de very first days, God made a man and a woman and put 'em in a house together to live. 'Way back in them days de woman was just as strong as de man and both of 'em did de same things. They useter get to fussin' 'bout who gointer do this and that and sometime they'd fight, but they was even balanced and neither one could whip de other one.

One day de man said to himself, "B'lieve Ah'm gointer go see God and ast Him for a li'l mo' strength so Ah kin whip dis 'oman and make her mind. Ah'm tired of de way things is." So he went on up to God.

"Good mawnin', Ole Father."

"Howdy man. Whut you doin' 'round my throne so soon dis mawnin'?"

"Ah'm troubled in mind, and nobody can't ease mah spirit 'ceptin' you."

God said, "Put yo' plea in de right form and Ah'll hear and answer."

"Ole Maker, wid de mawnin' stars glitterin' in yo' shinin' crown, wid de dust from yo' footsteps makin' worlds upon worlds, wid de blazin' bird we call de sun flyin' out of yo' right hand in de mawnin' and consumin' all day de flesh and blood of stump-black darkness, and comes flyin' home every evenin' to rest on yo' left hand, and never once in all yo' eternal years, mistood de left hand for de right, Ah ast you *please* to give me mo' strength than dat woman you give me, so Ah kin make her mind. Ah know you don't want to be always comin' down way past de moon and stars to be straightenin' her out, and it's got to be done. So give me a li'l mo' strength, Ole Maker, and Ah'll do it."

"All right, Man, you got mo' strength than woman."

So de man run all de way down de stairs from Heben till he got home. He was so anxious to try his strength on de woman dat he couldn't take his time. Soon's he got in de house, he hollered "Woman! Here's yo' boss. God done tole me to handle you in which ever way Ah please. Ah'm yo' boss."

De woman flew to fightin' 'im right off. She fought 'im frightenin', but he beat her. She got her wind and tried 'im agin, but he whipped her agin. She got herself together and made de third try on him vigorous, but he beat her every time. He was so proud he could whip 'er at last dat he just crowed over her and made her do a lot of things she didn't like. He told her, "Long as you obey me, Ah'll be good to yuh, but every time yuh rear up, Ah'm gointer put plenty wood on yo' back and plenty water in yo' eyes."

De woman was so mad, she went straight up to Heben and stood befo' de Lawd. She didn't waste no words. She said, "Lawd, Ah come befo' you mighty mad t'day. Ah want back my strength and power Ah useter have."

"Woman, you got de same power you had since de beginnin'."

"Why is it, then, dat de man kin beat me now and he useter couldn't do it?"

"He got mo' strength than he useter have. He come and ast me for it and Ah give it to 'im. Ah gives to them that ast, and you ain't never ast me for no mo' power."

"Please, suh, God, Ah'm astin' you for it now. Jus' gimme de same as you give him."

God shook his head. "It's too late now, woman. Whut Ah give, Ah never take back. Ah give him mo' strength than you and no matter how much Ah give you, he'll have mo'."

De woman was so mad, she wheeled around and went on off. She went straight to de devil and told him what had happened.

He said, "Don't be dis-incouraged, woman. You listen to me and you'll come out mo' than conqueror. Take dem frowns out yo' face and turn round and go right on back to Heben and ast God to give you dat bunch of keys hangin' by de mantel-piece. Then you bring 'em to me and Ah'll show you what to do wid 'em."

So de woman climbed back up to Heben agin. She was mighty tired, but she was more out-done than she was tired, so she climbed all night long and got back up to Heben agin. When she got befo' de throne, butter wouldn't melt in her mouf.

"O Lawd and Master of de rainbow, Ah know yo' power. You never make two mountains without you put a valley in between. Ah know you kin hit a straight lick wid a crooked stick."

"Ast for whut you want, woman."

"God, gimme dat bunch of keys hangin' by yo' mantel-piece."

"Take 'em."

So de woman took de keys an hurried on back to de devil wid 'em. There was three keys on de bunch. Devil say, "See dese three keys? They got mo' power in 'em than all de strength de man kin ever git if you handle 'em right. Now dis first big key is to de do' of de kitchen, and you know a man always favors his stomach. Dis second one is de key to de bedroom, and he don't like to be shut out from dat neither, and dis last key is de key to de cradle, and he don't want to be cut off from his generations at all. So now you take dese keys and go lock up everything and wait till he come to you. Then don't you unlock nothin' until he use his strength for yo' benefit and yo' desires."

De woman thanked 'im and tole 'im, "If it wasn't for you, Lawd knows whut us po' women folks would do."

She started off, but de devil halted her. "Jus' one mo' thing: Don't go home braggin' 'bout yo' keys. Jus' lock up everything and say nothin' until you git asked. And then don't talk too much."

De woman went on home and did like de devil tole her. When de man come home from work, she was settin' on de porch singin' some song 'bout "Peck on de wood make de bed go good."

When de man found de three doors fastened what useter stand wide open, he swelled up like pine lumber after a rain. First thing he tried to break in, cause he figgered his strength would overcome all obstacles. When he saw he couldn't do it, he ast de woman, "Who locked dis do'?"

She tole 'im, "Me."

"Where did you git de key from?"

"God give it to me."

He run up to God and said, "God, woman got me locked 'way from my vittles, my bed, and my generations, and she say you give her the keys."

God said, "I did, Man, Ah give her de keys, but de devil showed her how to use 'em!"

"Well, Ole Maker, please gimme some keys jus' lak 'em so she can't git de full control."

"No, Man, what Ah give Ah give. Woman got de key."

"How kin Ah know 'bout my generations?"

"Ast de woman."

So de man come on back and submitted hisself to de woman and she opened de doors.

He wasn't satisfied, but he had to give in. 'Way after while he said to de woman, "Le's us divide up. Ah'll give you half of my strength if you lemme hold de keys in my hands."

De woman thought dat over, so de devil popped and tol her, "Tell 'im, naw. Let 'im keep his strength and you keep yo' keys."

So de woman wouldn't trade wid 'im and de man had to mortgage his strength to her to live. And dat's why de man makes and de woman takes. You men is still braggin' 'bout yo' strength and de women is sittin' on de keys and lettin' you blow off till she git ready to put de bridle on you.

B. Moseley looked over at Mathilda and said, "You just like a hen in de barnyard. You cackle so much, you give de rooster de blues."

Mathilda looked over at him archly and quoted.

Stepped on a pin, de pin bent
And dat's de way de story went.

—FLORIDA FOLKLORE

"I WAS HAPPY AS A SINGLE MAN in a city with a twelve-to-one ratio of women to men. I was used to staying out whenever I liked and as late as I liked. But when I got married, my personal freedom was curbed. I had to account for my time, and that sometimes made me feel like I was six years old. But my wife demanded it. And, more to the point, she deserved no less. So if I go out for a drink with the boys and I see that I am going to be late, I call her. And I let her know where I can be reached. It's the right thing to do. Plus, it saves a lot of grief." —MICHAEL B., AGE TWENTY-NINE, EXECUTIVE ASSISTANT TO A GOVERNMENT OFFICIAL, NEW YORK CITY

THE HEN KNOWS WHEN IT IS DAY-BREAK, BUT ALLOWS THE ROOSTER TO MAKE THE ANNOUNCE-MENT.

—ASHANTI PROVERB

CELEBRATING
LOVE

ADMITTEDLY THERE IS a fine line between keeping love alive and celebrating love. The reason, of course, is that one of the best ways to keep love alive is to find ways to celebrate it. But no matter how narrow the distinction, it is still a real distinction, for in keeping love alive one reflects occasionally on the bleaker side of love, if only to learn and grow by reviewing those experiences.

Celebrating love is joy unfettered. There is a buoyancy and an exuberance that is transforming and that enables one to transcend the casual brutalities of the everyday world. In this section, I have included the love song to end all love songs—the Song of Solomon—as well as celebrity reflections on how love lights up a life by the likes of Sammy Davis, Jr., and the actress Halle Berry.

Food is also a wonderful way to celebrate love, feeding each other a sensuous Ethiopian meal or having a favorite dish together. For the poet Nikki Giovanni, that love dish is a special omelet. And in this chapter there are hosannas, in prose and poetry, to the physical expressions of love—of the caress, of the taste, of the sweetness and oneness of feeling that permeates one's entire body, mind, and soul in the celebration of true love.

Ten Ways to Celebrate Love

1. Renew your wedding vows in a spiritual setting.

2. Commemorate by remembering and talking about various firsts—first date, first kiss, first lovemaking—every month over a romantic dinner.

3. Revisit the place of your first date, first kiss, first lovemaking.

4. Write love letters to each other and put them in places where they will be found unexpectedly—jacket pockets, purses, in a book he is reading. I know one person who taped a love note under the lid of the toilet seat, which was quite a morning surprise.

5. Find physical things—eyes, teeth, hands, shoulders, clothing, scents—for which you can compliment your partner. Compliment him or her in the morning before going to work. Call just before lunch and compliment him or her on something else, and again in the afternoon. When the two of you meet at the end of the day, give your partner a big sloppy kiss and say how much you love him or her.

6. Travel together, even if it's just to a mound of earth in the backyard where you can hold hands and watch the sunset together. Of course, if you can escape to the Bahamas, that's good, too.

7. Write your partner a letter of encouragement and support about some goal, professional or personal, he or she is trying to achieve. Express your faith in him that he can achieve that goal and note the progress he has already made.

8. Leave flowers and a homemade heart on the kitchen table for no particular reason. (P.S., If you have children, don't be shy. It's good for children to see their parents acting like this toward each other.)

9. Put an ad in the personal-messages section of your paper. It can declare your love for your partner or simply be a tongue-in-cheek description of yourself and a description of your partner as the object of your desires. When the ad is published, casually bring it to your partner's attention.

10. Is there a particularly odious household duty that is your partner's responsibility? Today do it for him or her. And, if you are the lucky partner, don't forget to say thank you when that trash mysteriously disappears or the dishes are magically clean.

IT'S important to reiterate your love

for your longtime partner. You can do this privately, with notes or sweet nothings whispered in his or her ear at home. Or you can declare your love publicly. That is, during a party or during dinner with friends, say out loud what you like about your partner. Couples complain about each other in public so often, so why not use the same forum to say nice things?

Another way, and a fun way, to praise in public is to ask friends to call your honey throughout the day. In the morning, just after he or she arrives at work, you might ask someone to end a mundane conversation, with, "Oh, by the way, Jeanette thinks you have beautiful eyes," and at noon, another friend might end his conversation with, "Oh, yes, I almost forgot, Jeanette wanted me to remind you that she married you because you make the tastiest fried chicken in the world." Corny, I know, but when you love someone, you don't keep that love to yourself. You want your friends to know. You want to share your feelings with the world.

—JEANETTE P., AGE FIFTY-FIVE, JOURNALIST, CHICAGO

Dark an' stormy may come de wedder;

I jines dis he-male an' dis she-male togedder.

Let none, but Him dat makes de thunder,

Put dis he-male and dis she-male asunder.

I darefor 'nounce you bofe de same.

Be good, go 'long, an' keep up yo' name.

De broomstick's jumped, de world not wide.

She's now yo' own. Salute yo' bride!

—SLAVE MARRIAGE TOAST

"My husband and I spent our honeymoon on Cape Cod a week before Christmas. It was bracing, but we both enjoy cold weather. When we tired of exploring the hard seashore, we'd dive into the nearest inn or restaurant, warming our hands with a mug of hot mulled cider. Then it was back to exploring: sweaters to buy, antiques, mufflers, rag dolls. Finally we wandered into a shop specializing in Christmas ornaments. Nothing appealed to us, and besides, the owner seemed a bit pushy. We were on our way out when she asked what brought us to Cape Cod. We told her that it was our honeymoon. She told us not to move and disappeared into a back room. She reappeared shortly with a wooden Christmas ornament in the shape of a heart. It was about the size of the palm of your hand, painted red, very rustic, with a primitive loopy calligraphy that read 'Much Love.' She gave it to us for free.

"After that we bought or made a Christmas ornament each year to celebrate our love: a ceramic baby shoe and drumming circus bear to symbolize the birth of our children, a reproduction of an Ashanti gold weight to symbolize the first year we celebrated Kwanzaa, a miniature dried red rose to celebrate our continuing passion for each other. We keep a list of our ornaments—what was bought when and what it symbolizes—and will pass them to our children, who will pass them to their children, who will pass them to their children."

—JOAN M., AGE FORTY-FIVE, HOUSEWIFE/WRITER, BOSTON

The Origin of Marriage

Once upon a time there were four young men who always hunted together in the forest and lived on what they caught or shot. In those days there were no other people on earth yet, and history does not relate whether those men were born from a woman or whether they were created by God when he decided to make the human race. We do know that those men knew nothing of women, for when they first saw one, they were most surprised.

People did not wear any clothes in those days, and all the men wore were arrows, which they stuck in their hair to have them handy for quick shots. When they saw the naked woman then, they debated together whether she was a human being like them or a different species. They could see that she had no arrows, so she never hunted, therefore she could not be human, she must be a different animal. Only one of the men disagreed with this conclusion and decided to go and look at her and talk to her. Somehow none of the men thought of shooting and eating her.

The hunter who went up to her discovered to his pleasure that she understood his question and could answer him: No, she had never tasted meat, she could not hunt, she ate only berries and grains, which she roasted over the fire. The men had never made a fire, and it frightened them, since they associated it with lightning and thunder. This man, however, was more attracted by the woman than he was afraid of the fire.

She had shaped clay pots and baked them over her fire so that they kept their shape and could hold water, grains, or milk. The man gave her a piece of his meat, which she roasted over the fire and then shared with him. He found this roast meat the tastiest he had ever had and wondered how he could ever have liked raw meat. She offered him porridge cooked from ground grains and boiled tubers with his meat, and he could not remember ever having had such a satisfying meal. He told the woman, when all his meat was finished, that he must go back to the bush and hunt some more game.

He found his three comrades in the veld (savannah) and told them everything about life with his woman. He suggested they, too, might come and live with her, but they declined: They did not feel like sharing their meat with anyone who was not a hunter and did not contribute to the stock of meat they thought they needed every day. Moreover they preferred a wandering life to sleeping in the same place every night. They feared there would soon be no game left in that place. So they said good-bye to their friend and wished him good luck with his woman. He wished them good hunting and they went off into the wilderness. They never came back, and in the end all three died somewhere in the wilds.

The husband-man went back to his wife with his meat, warmed his hands over the fire, and reflected on the goodness of married life. They found a sheltered home in a cave, and there their children were born. He lived to see his grandchildren, and when he died, he was buried properly and not forgotten. But life went on after him.

—South Africa

"I met my husband in the off season on Oak Bluffs, a cozy neighborhood on Martha's Vineyard, an island just off the coast of Massachusetts, where blacks have been summering for generations. It's quiet in the fall, and we had independently gone up there to meditate, to think about new directions for our lives, and to enjoy the crisp salt sea air of autumn.

"When we first laid eyes on each other, we knew we were destined to get married. His grandparents owned a house on the island, and he had visited there every summer his whole life. He showed me around. He picked up from the ground a twig the length of his forearm and told me how he and his younger brother would fix twigs with string or a rubber band and pretend to be Indians hunting with bows and arrows. He playfully held the twig like a bow and let loose an imaginary arrow at my heart. He accompanied me back to the inn where I was staying, carrying the stick with him. A teddy bear with a violet ribbon around its neck sat on the fireplace mantel in the living room. He removed the ribbon, tied it into a bow near the top of the stick, and, using a plain ballpoint pen, wrote the words 'Oak Bluffs, Martha's Vineyard,' then handed it to me, saying simply, 'A souvenir.' I couldn't have been happier had he given me a jeweled scepter.

"We were married on the island a year later, and our marriage has been filled with much happiness, loving friends, three children. And although the stick disappeared during one of our many moves as we relocated during my husband's frequent promotions, we always returned to the island, spending August there.

"On our twenty-fifth wedding anniversary we had a real southern celebration—lots of food, music, laughing, and dancing. Among the many gifts was a baton-shaped object. Judging from the crinkled wrapping paper, the gift giver hadn't bothered to put the object into a box. Though that present caught my eye first, I opened it last. The first thing I saw when I peeled back the paper was a lavender bow, and as I continued peeling, I saw the letters, O-A-K. It turns out that because of our frequent moves, my husband had put the stick in our safe-deposit box so that it wouldn't get lost. He glanced at the stick and then looked at me with tears in his eyes. I opened my mouth to speak, and cried."

—CAROLYN S., AGE FIFTY-FIVE, HOUSEWIFE, PHILADELPHIA

"I am black, but beautiful...." Those biblical words from the "Song of Solomon" to the beloved Queen of Sheba have resonated throughout the black community for generations. But let us tinker with these words of antiquity. Let us say, "I am black, *and* beautiful" or "I am beautiful *because* I am black." And let us not just sing the praises of the ebony queen, Sheba—let us sing songs to the beauty of all our black queens around the world and throughout all time. Let us sing to them regardless of looks, regardless of age. Let us sing to their timeless beauty and eternal elegance. Let us sing a Song of Solomon.

You have ravished my heart, my sister,
            my bride,
        you have ravished my heart with a
        glance of your eyes,
        with one jewel of your necklace.
How sweet is your love, my sister, my
            bride!
        how much better is your love than
            wine,
        and the fragrance of your oils than
            any spice!
Your lips distill nectar, my bride;
        honey and milk are under your
            tongue;
        the scent of your garments is like the scent of Lebanon.
A garden locked is my sister, my bride,
        a garden locked, a fountain sealed.
Your shoots are an orchard of pomegrantes
        with all choicest fruits,
        henna with nard,
nard and saffron, calamus and cinnamon,
        with all trees of frankincense,
        myrrh and aloes,
        with all chief spices—
a garden fountain, a well of living
        water,
        and flowering streams from Lebanon.

—SONG OF SOLOMON, CHAPTER 4, VERSES 9–17

"One of the truest pictures of love is 'Anniversary,' by Ernie Barnes," says David Hodge, owner of the American Roots Art Gallery in Queens, NY. But what is it in that painting that would make David say that? Could it be the single rose in a vase on the cocktail table? Or the bottle of wine next to it? Perhaps it is the 1930s vintage radio from which, one imagines, romantic strains of Sarah Vaughan or Ella Fitzgerald waft into the cozy living room. It is all of the above, and more. The couple is ballroom-dancing, alone, in their living room. The beatific expressions on their faces indicate that they are lost in their own world, lost in their love. Their love is a love that needs no audience, that doesn't depend on display or the affirmation of others. Theirs is a love that needs no occasion for its expression. It is a molten love, a true love, an eternal love.

"When you're a single guy and you finish that show, no matter how loudly people applaud for you or how many of them you have up to your place afterwards, sooner or later everybody else goes home. You've got nobody to give you security, nobody to root for, nobody rooting for you. You've got no reason for doing the hundred and one things you do automatically when you're in love and you marry someone." —SAMMY DAVIS, JR.

I love Black men for their incredible strength in the face of rage, the racism and the rancor they must face on a daily basis.... Like millions of Black women, I know the special joy of marriage to a strong Black man with whom you share the same struggle. Only a Black man can truly understand the fight and the plight of our people. For me, that fight is made infinitely easier because of David. When I see him across the room, or wake up and see his face, I'm always renewed because I never have to explain myself or my feelings to him. He understands my pain because it is his pain; he understands my struggle because it is his struggle. What bond can be more powerful? What love can be more

"I had been working for years to get the promotion. Then a rumor circulated that I had won, and that it would just be a matter of time before my promotion would be announced. I tried not to jinx it, but nonetheless I felt a current of excitement when my boss's secretary called me into his office. Unfortunately it was to tell me the company had passed me over.

"When I returned to my desk, I saw my husband had called to remind me that he was going to a big basketball game that evening. I called to tell him that I hadn't gotten the promotion. I told him that while I was disappointed, I was basically okay, so he should go to the big game. Besides, I was tired and planning to turn in early. There was silence on his end of the line, and then he said, 'I love you very much.'

"When I left work, my husband was waiting for me in the lobby. He gave me a long hug, a soft kiss, and held my hand as we left the building. We walked hand in hand down the quiet streets. We sat shoulder to shoulder on a park bench, where we fed the ducks in a nearby pond. I talked and he listened. And then there were long stretches of blissful quiet where just knowing he was there was a comfort. My husband is not much bigger than I am, and as for his muscle, well, let's just say that in college they called him spaghetti arms. But that night, as I lay in his arms, I felt as calm and secure and protected as if I were nestled in the arms of Hercules."

—DARLA R., AGE TWENTY-NINE, ACCOUNT EXECUTIVE, CLEVELAND

BLACK LOVE

Black love, provide the adequate electric
for what is lapsed and lenient in us now.

Rouse us from blur. Call us.

Call adequately the postponed corner brother.
And call our man in the pin-stripe suiting and restore
him to his abler logic; to his people.

Call to the shattered sister and repair her
in her difficult hour, narrow her fever.

Call to the Elders—
our customary grace and further sun
loved in the Long-ago, loathed in the Lately;
a luxury of languish and of rust.

Appraise, assess our Workers in the Wild, lest they
descend to malformation and to undertow.

Black love, define and escort our young, be means and
redemption, discipline.

Nourish our children—proud, strong
little men upright-easy:
quick
flexed
little stern-warm historywomen....
I see them in Ghana, Kenya, in the city of Dar-es-
Salaam, in Kalamazoo, Mound Bayou, in Chicago.

Lovely loving children
with long soft eyes.

Black love, prepare us for all interruptions;
assaults, unwanted pauses; furnish for leavings and
          for losses

Just come out Blackly glowing!

On the ledges—in the lattices—against the failing
          light of
candles that stutter,
and in the chop and challenge of our apprehension—
be
the Alwayswonderful of this world.

—GWENDOLYN BROOKS

"There is a power that Black sexuality exudes that is as powerful as the sun shining. People in Hollywood want to embrace it, but they also want to contain and control it.... But you cannot control where the sun shines."

—DEBBIE ALLEN

"The most romantic aspect of Ethiopian

food is sharing food from a communal plate and feeding each other. When I was young, my parents would take us on a picnic trip and we would stop for lunch and park ourselves under a tree and eat together. My father would roll up the Watt sauce (a spicy Ethiopian sauce for meats) in an injera (a pancake-like bread with a spongy consistency that is eaten with different sauces and that is a main staple in Ethiopia) and feed my mom and she would do the same for him. He called her nefse ('my life'). They would both sing songs in the car while driving to our destination." —RACHEL YOHANNES, FOUNDER OF AFRI-Q ETHIOPIAN BARBECUE SAUCES

RACHEL YOHANNES'S WATT SAUCE WITH BEEF

(ADJUSTED FOR AMERICAN TASTE AND DIET)

1 cup red onions, chopped
½ cup (1 stick) butter
1 cup red pepper (Berbere in Ethiopia)
¼ cup red wine
2 pounds beef, cut into cubes
½ teaspoon ground cardamom
½ teaspoon ground ginger
¼ teaspoon black cumin
½ teaspoon ground cloves
¼ teaspoon garlic powder
Salt

Over a low flame, sauté the onions with the butter until browned. Add the red pepper and stir gently. Add the wine and keep stirring. Add the meat and the spices and a touch of salt. Simmer on low heat for 20 to 30 minutes, or until thickened. Serve with pita bread or couscous as a substitute for *injera*.

LOVE SONG

I painted my eyes with black antimony.
I girded myself with amulets.

I will satisfy my desire—
You, my slender boy.
I walk behind the wall.
I have covered my bosom.
I shall knead colored clay.
I shall paint the house of my friend,
O my slender boy.
I shall take my piece of silver.
I will buy silk.
I will gird myself with amulets.
I will satisfy my desire,
The horn of antimony in my hand,
O my slender boy!

—BAGAIRMI PEOPLE, AFRICA

A
WOMAN'S STRENGTH IS A MULTITUDE OF WORDS.

—African (Hausa) proverb

I Wrote a Good Omelet

I wrote a good omelet...and ate a hot poem...
after loving you

Buttoned my car...and drove my coat home...in the
        rain...
after loving you

I goed on red...and stopped on green...floating somewhere
        in between...
being here and being there...
after loving you

I rolled my bed...turned down my hair...slightly confused
        but...I don't care...
Laid out my teeth...and gargled my gown...then I stood
        ...and laid me down...
to sleep...
after loving you

—Nikki Giovanni

NIKKI GIOVANNI'S OMELETS FOR TWO

You will need a shallow skillet, a fork, a good chunk of unsalted butter, a pinch of rosemary (preferably fresh), one clove of garlic, peeled, a sprig of fresh peppermint leaves, about a quarter cup of champagne, and four eggs.

First, soak your mint sprigs overnight in a splash of champagne (even New York State will be all right for this).

That evening take the four eggs from the refrigerator and let come to not quite room temperature but a bit of a sweat, just a hint of water forming on the oval will be fine.

In a wonderfully beautiful bowl that is not too deep nor too shallow but, well, committed to containing the eggs and able to hold them in even during a good solid workout with the fork...break the eggs. Never rush a breaking egg. Enjoy the sight of the egg coming to you, listen closely for its first touch with the bowl; there must be, of course, no odor but there should be the revelation of the yolk falling yet holding itself together as it nestles in the bowl. Repeat this three more times.

Take the skillet and put it on the stove. Turn the heat on as low as possible. I am aware that many people think high heat is good for omelets but omelets make their own heat and should therefore be slowly coaxed to the temperature you desire. Slide, not glob, the butter into the skillet. Take the garlic clove and let it interact with the butter as the butter is melting. You, in the meantime, take the fork and begin whisking the eggs. I know, you are now saying, I should have gotten a whisk out in the first place. Wrong. You need a fork because we hold a fork differently from a whisk. We have more respect for a fork. And respect is everything to omelets. Whisk the eggs with the fork one hundred and twenty times. Just count that out. By then your butter will have melted and your garlic will have released its age-old magic. Remove the garlic from the skillet and gently slide the eggs in.

At this time it is good to do something else so as not to rush the eggs. Go to your refrigerator and bring back the sprigs of peppermint leaves. Drain off the champagne into a small white-wine glass. Drink this. Then return to the stove to turn the eggs over. Don't flip but gently coax the eggs over. Add the rosemary. Turn off the heat. In your warmed plate place the omelet. Add the peppermint sprigs for color. Call sweetly to your...well, guest. Take the fork. One for you. One for him. One for you. One for him. One for you. One for him.

All gone.

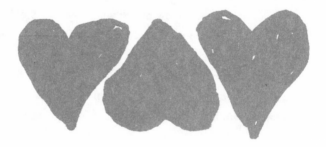

YOU COME TO ME

you come to me
during the cool hours
of the day bringing
the sun; if you come
at midnight, or at two
in the morning, you come
always bringing the sun;
the taste of your sweetness
permeates my lips and my hair
with the lingering sweetness of Harlem
with the lingering sweetness of Africa
with the lingering sweetness of freedom;
woman, eye want to see
your breast brown and bared,
your nippled eyes staring,
aroused-hard and lovely;
woman, eye want to see
the windows of your suffering
washed clean of this terrible pain
we endure together;
woman, eye want to see
your song filled with joy,
feel the beat of your laughter;
woman, black beautiful woman,
eye want to see
your black graceful body
covered with the sweat of our love
with your dancer's steps to music
moving rhythmically, panther like
across the African veldt;
woman, eye want to see you
naked, always in your natural beauty;
woman, eye want to see you
proud; in your native land

—QUINCY TROUPE

THE IRONY about marriage is that

you want to do two contradictory things: You want to get to know each other better, and yet you have to maintain the spark and mystery that attracted you to your partner in the first place. One way my wife and I have tried to harness these contradictory impulses is to keep a romantic scrap book together. Our first book was a blue two-dollar looseleaf binder, but when we got more money, we bought books made of leather. It doesn't really matter, though, what you use. It is truly the thought that counts. We use the scrap book to document our special moments. For instance, we were in our room at a ski lodge not long ago, just after a good, long day on the slopes. I made sure that our fireplace was roaring, and that we had a little cognac on hand. My wife and I were sitting on the daybed, her legs lying across mine. I had a chocolate bar and asked her if she wanted some. When she said yes, I carefully opened the wrapper, broke the bar in half. I put one half back in the wrapper. I then said "Here" and put the remaining half between my teeth. She nibbled at it until she reached my lips and then we kissed passionately. With the moon reflecting off the snow, and the golden light of the fire and the cognac, it was a very special moment for us, an evening, I might add, that ended not with sex, but that melted into hours of hugging and snuggling and kissing—sometimes hard, sometimes soft—until we fell asleep in each other's arms in front of the fire. When we returned home, I put the candy wrapper in our scrap book to remind us of our special time in Vermont.

— ALAN M., AGE SIXTY, CHEF, SPRINGFIELD, MA

"I WAS
IN LOVE
WITH
HARLEM
LONG
BEFORE
I GOT
THERE."

—LANGSTON HUGHES

"JAZZ IS...THE SENSUOUSNESS OF ROMANCE IN OUR DIALECT."

—WYNTON MARSALIS

Ancient Memories

Ancient Memories!
>> Before History.
>>>> Before Time.
>>>>>> Before Earth
>>>>>>>> and Stars
>>>>>>>>>> and Galaxies.

Before God Spoke the Word
>>>>>> or Declared Light
>>>>>>>> or Moved as Love.

In the Primordial,
>>>> Formless,
>>>>>>> Presubstantiated
>>> Womb of God!

We Were

>>> We Are

>>> We Forever!

—Nirvana Reginald Gayle

"Defying a history of horror and a now-ness of brutality, Black men glisten with strength, sparkle with wit and glow with love. I am the daughter, the mother, the grand-mother, the sister, the friend and the beloved of wonderful Black men and that makes my heart glad."

—MAYA ANGELOU

"MY MEALS ARE

so romantic now because my husband, Herbert, does all the shopping and cooking. It's really romantic for me to be in bed in the morning and he comes upstairs and he brings a rose from our garden and puts it in a glass of cool water. I'm lying there with my eyes closed and he takes the rose from the water and touches my nose with it. Then for breakfast he serves me broiled salmon or omelet grits with chopped garlic and rye toast. Sometimes it's sardine omelets. (You really gotta' love someone to kiss them after that.) It's very simple and very romantic.

—SYLVIA WOODS, QUEEN OF SOUL FOOD AND FOUNDER OF SYLVIA'S RESTAURANT

"'I' CANNOT REACH
FULFILLMENT WITH-
OUT 'THOU.' THE SELF
CANNOT BE SELF
WITHOUT OTHER
SELVES. SELF-CONCERN
WITHOUT OTHER-
CONCERN IS LIKE A
TRIBUTARY THAT HAS
NO OUTWARD FLOW."

—DR. MARTIN LUTHER KING, JR.